Managing Managers

Human Resource Management in Action Series

Edited by Brian Towers

Managing Managers

Strategies and Techniques for Human Resource Management

ED SNAPE, TOM REDMAN AND
GREG J. BAMBER

First published 1994

Blackwell Publishers
108 Cowley Road
Oxford OX4 1JF
UK

238 Main Street
Cambridge, Massachusetts 02142
USA

British Library Cataloguing in Publication Data
A CIP catalogue record for this book is available from the British Library.

Library of Congress Cataloging-in-Publication Data
Snape, Ed, 1957
    Managing managers: strategies and techniques for human resource management /
Ed Snape, Tom Redman, and Greg J. Bamber.
        p.   cm. – (Human resource management in action)
    Includes bibliographical
    references and index.
    ISBN 0-631-18675-1 (pbk.)
    1. Assessment centers (Personnel management procedure).   2. Executives –
Recruiting.   3. Executives – Rating of.   4. Executives – Training of.
I. Redman, Tom, 1952–.   II. Bamber. Greg, 1949–.   III. Title.   IV. Series.
HF5549.5.A78S64   1994
658.4'07124 – dc20
                                                                    93-1480
                                                                    CIP

Typeset in 11 on 13 pt Plantin by Best-set Typesetter Ltd, Hong Kong
Printed in Great Britain by Page Brothers (Norwich) Ltd

This book is printed on acid-free paper

Contents

Boxed Exhibits

Foreword

Business as an institution and careers in business both experienced an enormous gain in social status during the 1980s. In part this was tied to political swings as Western economies became increasingly disillusioned with the ability of government to solve social problems; it also seems, in retrospect, to have been related to a resurgence of materialism and a philosophy of greed. This was a decade of great expansion in business schools and MBA programmes; of the view that management and managers should replace mere administrators in arts organizations, hospitals or national parks; of the public's fascination with high executive salaries and office intrigue; and of the need to be on the 'fast track'.

But this was only one – albeit glamorous – part of the story in the 1980s. Another part was the growing belief within companies that managers and what they do were crucial ingredients in organization performance and thus should be looked at more critically. On the positive side, this led to advances in managerial selection, career development, performance compensation, and planning. Less positive were the advent of layoffs among managers and a decline in morale.

A group of scholars, in the late eighties, sensing that both trends were taking place, organized a cross-national working group to document the changing characteristics of managerial employment. Greg Bamber and Ed Snape were part of that group and contributed some of the early research documenting how the terms and conditions of managerial employment were being redefined. In this book, *Managing Managers: Strategies and Techniques for Human Resource Management*, Snape and Bamber and their colleague Tom Redman continue that research tradition.

Studying managers as human resources during the 1980s was not an easy task. Studies had been done on managerial careers, how managers make decisions, and how managers perform their jobs, but the view of manager as worker was not widely acknowledged in academic circles. Consequently, working group members were limited to studying developments as they were taking place. As *Managing Managers* clearly shows, however, currently there is an extensive literature on the subject, which Snape, Redman and Bamber have summarized skilfully.

Students of human resource management will find this an excellent introduction to emerging developments in the field. Practitioners, who are themselves creating those trends, and in fact are the subjects of those developments, can see in this book how the human resource practices dealing with managers fit together.

Myron Roomkin,
Professor of Human Resource Management,
Kellogg School of Management,
Northwestern University

Series Editor's Preface

Managers, as foremen a generation ago, may be in danger of becoming part of the 'forgotten' within the organization or, as the authors tell us in this volume, of suffering from 'benign neglect'; nor is this neglect in the abstract context of the organization but seen to be embedded in the actual behaviour of senior management.

Organizations, and those who are responsible for their direction, must clearly try to see their managers in a much clearer light. This is largely because there still remains a glaring need to improve the overall performance of British management – as the authors remind us – and this underperformance still regularly attracts critical comparative studies. The contexts are also tightening. Organizations are increasingly assailed by changes and improvements in products, productive processes, technology and markets which require greater flexibility from them as organizations and from the people who work for them. As for managers, the human consequences are great. They are increasingly required to work to much higher demands and greater stress to ensure job security – albeit for potentially greater rewards in pay and achievement.

The authors also tell us that there are now fewer managers, as organizations become 'flatter', removing hierarchical layers. Their scarcity underlines their value as an important human resource requiring careful attention to their selection, performance, appraisal, rewards and development: that is, the practice of competent, professional human resource management.

In sum, the theme of this book is that organizations neglect their managers at their peril. A careful reading of its pages should help organizations avoid such a fate.

Brian Towers
Strathclyde Business School

Acknowledgements

In a team effort such as this book, there are many people to thank. Here, we mention just a few of them.

In particular, we would like to acknowledge the substantial contribution of Val Bamber to chapters 4 and 5. Thanks are due to the following people, who read and commented on the whole or parts of the manuscript: Pat Allatt, Yasuo Kuwahara, Cliff Lockyer, Noah Meltz, Trevor Rigby, Myron Roomkin, Mairi Steele, Peter Wickens and Sharon Winocur. As series editor, Brian Towers gave us a great deal of helpful advice and encouragement. Thanks are also due to Richard Burton of Blackwell's, and to Stephen Ball. All errors and omissions are, of course, down to us.

We owe a debt to our colleagues, past and present, for providing each of us with a stimulating and helpful work environment. Above all, we thank our families.

1

Introduction:
The Challenges of
the 1990s and Beyond

This book is concerned with the way in which organizations manage
their managers. In recent years, there has been growing recognition
of the importance of using people's talents to the full if organizational
goals are to be met. However, much of this discussion has focused on
employees in general. Whilst we are in sympathy with those who
suggest that organizations must develop and utilize the talents of all
their employees, managerial staff are a particularly important group,
and managing them effectively is likely to be a critical ingredient of
organizational success. Hence this book.

The book explores the challenges facing organizations in managing
their managers, and shows how they are meeting these challenges.
We examine the impact of the changing corporate environment, and
we emphasize that policies and practices are continually developing.
What emerges is a picture of considerable change and innovation.

Whilst we focus mainly on the experience of organizations operating
in the UK and other English-speaking countries, the importance
of European integration and the internationalization of business is
reflected throughout the book. Furthermore, many of the themes
and approaches covered are of equal importance to organizations in
other countries.

The book is aimed particularly at human resource management
(HRM) specialists and senior managers with responsibilities for the
management of managers, but it will be of interest to any manager
seeking a guide to developments in this area, and also to students on
MBA, specialist postgraduate and advanced undergraduate courses.

In this introductory chapter, we argue that the performance

of managers is critical to the performance of organizations and of
the economy as a whole. We review some of the key challenges
facing organizations in the 1990s, and examine the implications
for managers. We discuss the importance of adopting a strategic
approach to HRM and provide a brief outline of the structure of the
rest of the book. In a postscript to the chapter, we discuss in detail
what we mean by the term 'manager'.

Is there a British management problem?

Since the late nineteenth century, Britain has been underperforming
relative to its main industrial competitors:

> Since around 1880, Britain's rate of growth of national income has
> been significantly lower – often less than half of – than those of its
> main competitors. At the same time, the growth rate of productivity
> (or output per worker) has been slower: again, often less than half
> those of competitor countries. . . . Finally, Britain's share of world
> trade in manufactures has declined, from about 40 per cent in 1880, to
> less than 7 per cent a century later. (Smith 1989: 55)

A variety of explanations have been put forward to explain this
relative economic decline, with governments, workers, trade unions,
bankers and management all receiving a share of the blame. Of
interest to us is the suggestion that Britain's economic decline can be
attributed, at least in part, to poor management.

A common argument is that the entrepreneurial vigour of Britain's
industrial revolution was dissipated once the second and third generation owners took control of their family businesses. Investment
and marketing opportunities were then neglected, and British industry eventually began to lag behind its competitors, as the latter-
day owners used their inherited fortunes to buy landed estates and
ape the gentry, rather than taking a close interest in business (Smith
1989: 188–9). This historic dash for respectability by the sons of the
early entrepreneurs illustrates, perhaps even explains, the British
disdain for manufacturing industry, with liberal education being
valued over science and technology, and with careers such as medicine, the law and the civil service being preferred over manufacturing (Wiener 1981).

Such themes have echoed down the last century. Alford argues that poor management emerges as an important weakness of the UK economy during the period 1945 to 1975:

> Inadequate cost-accounting practices, poor marketing, bad industrial relations, slow rates of technical innovation: all these were revealed as major weaknesses in comparisons drawn between Britain and her major competitors. (1988: 64–5)

Some have suggested that such inadequacies reflect poor management education and training, and concern has been expressed at the relatively low level of formal educational qualifications among British managers (Mant 1977; Constable and McCormick 1987; Handy 1987; see chapter 4). British management have also been accused of lacking an appreciation of strategic management, and of being prone to 'short-termism' (Storey and Sisson 1990: 63).

Such a critical view of the contribution of management to Britain's relative economic decline has not gone unchallenged, and some have argued that British management is now tackling many of its previous shortcomings. Management education and training appears to have improved in recent years (see chapter 4), and there is evidence that British management is becoming more meritocratic (see box 1.1).

Many commentators have pointed to an economic miracle since the advent of the Conservative government in 1979, with managers finally confronting the overstaffing and inefficiency which had characterized much of British manufacturing industry. According to this view, economic policy and new employment laws have weakened the trade unions and restored management's right to manage, contributing to a marked improvement in productivity growth in British manufacturing in the late 1980s (Hanson 1991).

Whilst many have challenged the notion that there was a fundamental and sustainable transformation in British industry during this period (Nolan 1989), substantial retrenchment did take place, and new working practices were introduced. There appeared to many to be a new managerial confidence and entrepreneurial spirit in the 1980s. Furthermore, the re-election of a Conservative government for a fourth term in 1992 suggested that the policies which underpinned the new-found managerial confidence of the 1980s would continue.

Whilst there is some debate on the extent to which the long-term underperformance of British manufacturing industry may be attributed to poor management, most would agree that the prospects for

Box 1.1   Social change in the boardroom: The classless society in the making?

Britain has long been characterized as a society divided by social class. Whilst industrial management has often been seen as a lower status career than, for example, the law, medicine, the civil service, or even academia, nevertheless senior management positions have in the past been seen as the preserve of a social elite. The tradition was for the chairmen of the largest companies and top civil servants to have attended one of the prestigious public schools and perhaps either Oxford or Cambridge University.

However, there were signs by the 1980s that things were changing. Whilst in 1979, 29 of the chairmen of the 50 largest industrial companies had been educated at a public (fee-paying) school, by 1989 this figure had fallen to 12. Over the same period, the number of top chairmen educated at grammar or other state-maintained schools rose from 14 to 27.

Thus, the indications are that British management was becoming more meritocratic by the 1960s, with most of these top managers being promoted through the middle-management ranks at that time. The education reforms of 1944 and changing social attitudes throughout the post-war era appear to be responsible. Mr Major's vision of a 'classless society' has much to recommend it, but it is important not to underestimate the achievements of earlier governments, both Conservative and Labour, in moving Britain towards that goal.

Source: *Financial Times*, 3/4 November 1990: 11.

a prosperous future rely on an improvement in managerial performance. The management of managers emerges as a key area and, as we shall argue throughout this book, there are signs that employers are realizing this. In the next two sections of this chapter, we examine some of the key challenges facing organizations and their managers in the coming decades.

Managing through change

Management, particularly in the public sector and in many large private-sector organizations, has traditionally been seen as a relatively secure occupation. It has often provided steady and to some extent predictable career progression. The individual manager's authority has been underpinned by the rules and operating procedures of the organization, and a growing number of 'managers' are technical specialists, often with little or no line-management responsibility. Thus, during the twentieth century, many managers have come to look more like the salaried bureaucrat than the independent entrepreneur or even the general foreman of the industrial revolution (Whyte 1960).

However, in more recent years there has been a move away from the relatively secure bureaucracy. The 'long boom' of the post-war era was drawing to a close by the early 1970s, as oil shocks and recurring recession meant that world markets were becoming more volatile. The rise of the newly industrialized countries means that competition is much tougher than hitherto. Customers have become more demanding, not only on price, but more particularly in terms of choice, quality, service and design. The pace of product and process innovation has quickened, and developments in technology are having a major impact on organizations and their managers.

Such developments have led organizations to search for new strategies and structures. Greater competition and more discerning customers in many markets mean that product and service quality are now high on the agenda, with quality certification and total quality management (TQM) emerging as key concerns (Wilkinson et al. 1991). Many companies are increasingly targeting their products at niche markets, rather than selling standard mass-produced goods. In consequence, there is a greater emphasis on flexible, responsive organizations, rather than on simply reaping economies of scale (McKinlay and Starkey 1992).

Public-sector organizations are facing parallel pressures. Constraints on public expenditure and growing demands on public services have led to a drive for greater efficiency. In Britain, the Conservative government's Citizen's Charter initiative has involved greater accountability to the public on quality and standards of service, and an attempt to create greater 'customer awareness' amongst staff. Market competition has been extended with the privatization and liberalization of former public-sector monopolies, and with the introduction of competitive tendering and market testing in much of the public sector. Private-sector management techniques have been introduced, for example with the health service reforms and the introduction of performance-related pay.

Stable bureaucracy is not necessarily the most efficient organizational form, especially in an era when creativity and flexibility are at a premium. Private- and public-sector organizations are attempting to make themselves more responsive to their customers and clients by decentralizing and delayering (Peters 1989; Kanter 1990; for some British examples see Arkin 1990).

All this poses important challenges for managers, and for those who manage them. More volatile markets mean that jobs are less secure, as evidenced by the managerial redundancies at major companies during the recession of the late 1980s and early 1990s. Managers are not immune from the impact of restructuring and recession, and the days are gone when many managers could count on a job for life.

Flatter managerial hierarchies may mean fewer managerial jobs and less scope for the traditional organizational career, so that job moves may increasingly be of the lateral or cross-organizational type. This may require innovative approaches to career management on the part of employers, and a more flexible attitude to their own career development on the part of managers themselves. There may also be implications for motivation and remuneration strategies, as it becomes more difficult to reward good performers with promotion.

The jobs that remain are likely to be more demanding, in terms of the span of control and the range of functions and skills required of the manager. In many organizations, line managers are now taking more responsibility for what were formerly specialist functions, such as quality control, engineering services and personnel, and the emphasis is now on all managers adopting a broader business perspective (Dopson and Stewart 1990; Storey 1992; see box 1.2). The implication is that managers require new skills, not only in technical areas, but in dealing with employees and customers, so that there is likely to be a requirement for training and development throughout the managerial career.

In future, there may be more emphasis on managers working in teams and on discrete projects (Wheatley 1992: 22). Greater employee involvement and 'empowerment' may demand a more participative management style (Wilkinson et al. 1991). Indeed, a possible lack of commitment to employee involvement and TQM amongst middle managers has been seen as a key barrier to the successful implementation of such schemes. According to a recent study:

Box 1.2 From 'production manager' to 'business manager': The changing managerial role

On the basis of interviews with 350 managers in 35 organizations during 1986–88, John Storey of Loughborough University suggests that the role of middle-level line managers had been changing in response to the competitive challenges of the 1980s.

His analysis distinguishes between commercially as opposed to technically orientated managers, and between proactive or reactive managers. This two-dimensional distinction gives rise to four role types:

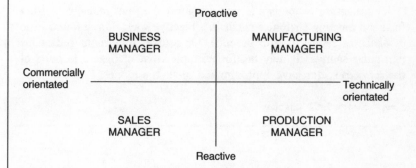

The *production manager* is the traditional role for many managerial jobs, concerned mainly with meeting given schedules, and keeping production going. Storey, however, argues that many organizations were seeking to transform this traditional role into the *manufacturing manager*. Here, the manager is still preoccupied primarily with technical aspects of production, but adopts a more proactive approach in seeking out ways of reducing costs, and improving efficiency and productivity. This may involve a reorganization, whereby former support functions, such as quality control, engineering, maintenance, and materials flow, are brought under the control of the manufacturing manager at the local level. In this respect, the role involves adopting responsibility for a wider range of functions and staff. The manager will now be more concerned with budgets and costs, and may be held accountable on this basis.

However, even this transformation is insufficient for some organizations, which have gone even further. They have developed the line manager's role into that of a *business manager*, who is expected to have a fuller commercial awareness of the organization, its customers or clients, and its competitive environment. The job performance of such a manager is expected to reflect this understanding, with an emphasis on continuous improvement in meeting customer needs.

In sum, Storey argues that the line manager's role has been shifting towards a more proactive and commercially orientated approach. As a senior line manager from the Longbridge plant of Austin Rover put it:

> Yes, there has been a massive shift! Fundamentally, we have moved from how a production man would run it to how a businessman would . . . that is, it is no longer just a question of meeting schedules, we now do that with monotonous regularity . . . (quoted in Storey 1992: 200)

Thus, the basic production manager responsibilities for schedules have not disappeared; they remain within the broader remit of the manager's role.

The diagram contains a fourth category, the sales manager, with a focus on meeting customer needs in a reactive way. Storey found little evidence of such a role in practice. Of course, this might reflect his particular sample. It may be, for example, that managers in parts of the services sector have approximated to such a model.

Source: Storey 1992: chapter 7.

[This is] . . . understandable given the potential impact some forms of [employee involvement] may have on the managerial role which, at one end of the spectrum, visualises managers as 'coaches' rather than 'cops', as facilitators rather than supervisors, or as people experts rather than technical experts. (Marchington et al. 1992: 38)

Some managers may experience difficulty in adapting to the new role, particularly if their own performance continues to be appraised in terms of traditional quantitative targets. The management of managers again emerges as a critical area.

Managers at all levels are increasingly being held accountable for both their own personal performance, and that of the unit for which they are responsible. Improvements in management information systems have provided senior management with the means to carry out such monitoring, and there is an attempt to link rewards more closely to performance, at both the individual and organizational level.

Managing under pressure

Given the above developments, it is hardly surprising that there has been a lively debate amongst academics and managers themselves on the extent to which managers are under increasing pressure in their jobs. Several studies have argued that there is growing disillusionment and disaffection amongst managers, with talk of 'burnout', 'professional suicide', and 'mid-career crisis' (Hunt 1986); the 'managerial menopause' (Davies and Deighan 1986); and the 'reluctant manager' (Goffee and Scase 1986; Scase and Goffee 1989).

One argument is that, traditionally, most managers saw their career as their primary interest in life. Single-income families were the norm, with the male as the breadwinner, and the wife providing the manager with the necessary domestic and emotional support. The rapid expansion of managerial hierarchies during this period meant that career ambitions were generally realizable. There was a 'psychological contract' between the manager, his family and the organization, involving a clear division of labour in the home, and a high level of commitment from the manager to the organization, in return for job security and career prospects (Whyte 1960; Scase and Goffee 1989).

This psychological contract has been threatened by many of the developments outlined in the previous section. Managerial workloads have increased, not least because there are often fewer managers to do the work. Many are taking on a broader range of responsibilities than previously, and are under greater pressure to perform. The level of discretion afforded to some managers in their work has declined, as technological change has de-skilled many managerial jobs, and allowed senior management to monitor the work of middle managers more closely. All this comes at a time when the number of job and promotion opportunities is being squeezed due to economic uncertainty and organizational delayering.

Not surprisingly, the argument goes, they are feeling the pressure. Middle and junior managers may feel themselves to be excluded from 'management'. As a middle manager explained to us about his organization:

> I think managers and staff are now far closer to each other than they are to management. That's a development I've seen over the years; managers and management used to be very close to each other.

The implication is that managers may react by becoming more 'detached' and 'instrumental' in their attitude to what is, after all, 'just a job' (Goffee and Scase 1986: 3). 'Organization man' (Whyte 1960) is replaced by the 'reluctant manager' (Scase and Goffee 1989), as individuals are less willing to prioritize work above domestic and leisure interests. The growing number of dual career couples, and changing social attitudes towards the domestic division of labour, further the development of such attitudes.

However, this pessimistic view of the predicament of managers has been challenged. Dopson and Stewart (1990) argue that it is not possible to generalize such a view. For example, whilst information technology may well have de-skilled some managers' jobs, many feel that it releases them from the burden of mundane tasks, 'empowering' them to do a more effective management job. A recent British Institute of Management (BIM) survey found that most managers had personal experience of organizational restructuring or delayering, and whilst this usually led to an increase in workload and responsibility, few saw such reorganizations as a threat to their current job or their future managerial career (Wheatley 1992). In many organizations the opportunities for promotion have declined, but managers are increasingly pursuing their careers by moving between organizations (see chapter 5).

Whilst performance may be under closer scrutiny, not all managers resent this. Many appear to welcome the challenge, feeling that they now have greater discretion and responsibility in their work, and are recognized by their employer as having a critical role to play in the success of the organization (Dopson and Stewart 1990: 13–14). Policies on performance management and performance-linked rewards may well contribute to this (see chapter 6).

In sum, change is at the top of the agenda, and whilst the implications are not wholly bleak, there are a number of key challenges for managers and for those who manage them. The following chapters provide a guide to the key issues, and a discussion of the ways in which organizations are responding.

Managing the managers: A strategic approach

There is a view, implicit in the approach of many organizations, that managers can look after themselves, and need less managing than do other employees. As Longenecker and Gioia put it:

senior managers seem typically to believe that managers are autono-
mous, self-starting, and self-directing individuals or they would not be
managers – a belief that governs their approach to managing their
managers. This belief also leads to dysfunctional attitudes such as
'benign neglect' and the 'let them sink or swim' mentality. (1991: 89)

For example, managers often receive little or no training for their
managerial role, and little real feedback from their superiors on their
job performance.

In fact, the complex, ambiguous and critical nature of most managerial jobs means that organizations cannot afford to let their managers 'sink or swim'; managerial performance is simply too important
for this. What is needed is a strategic approach to their management.
As we shall see in the following chapters, there is evidence that some
organizations are moving away from the 'benign neglect' approach,
but we also show that in many cases more could be done.

Devanna et al. (1984) argue that the various elements of human
resource management (HRM) should fit together as a coherent whole
(see box 1.3). Their 'HRM cycle' consists of four 'generic functions':
selection, appraisal, development and rewards. The aim is to manage
individual and organizational performance by selecting managers
with the appropriate skills and attitudes, by appraising their performance, and then motivating them through the management of rewards and developing them as appropriate. This feeds back into
performance, and possibly also into future selection decisions. Of
course, the HRM cycle is not a closed system, and performance is
also influenced by the strategy and structure of the organization, and
by the corporate environment.

The book is structured around the HRM cycle. Chapter 2 examines the recruitment and selection of managers, looking at recruitment channels and selection methods, and examining developments
in recruitment and selection practices. Chapter 3 discusses the
appraisal of managerial performance, examining new developments
in the appraisal of managers, and offering guidance on the design of
appraisal systems. Chapter 4 outlines the different approaches to
the training and development of managers, and reviews recent debates and developments such as the Management Charter Initiative.
Chapter 5 links together the themes of development and rewards, by
discussing approaches to the management of managers' careers in the
context of changing organizational structures and developing human
resource (HR) strategies. Chapter 6 looks at management remunera-

Box 1.3 The human resource management cycle

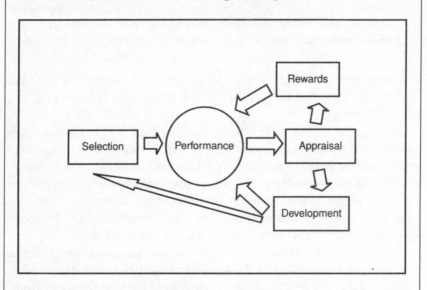

Source: Mary Anne Devanna, Charles J. Fombrun and Noel M. Tichy, A framework for strategic human resource management. In Charles J. Fombrun, Noel M. Tichy and Mary Anne Devanna (eds), *Strategic Human Resource Management* (New York: John Wiley and Sons, 1984), figure 3.2, page 41. Copyright © 1984 by John Wiley & Sons, Inc. Reprinted with permission.

tion, with particular emphasis on attempts to attract, retain and motivate able managers through reward strategies.

In view of the growing employer interest in equal opportunities, we felt that it would be useful to provide a systematic discussion of such issues in a single chapter. Hence chapter 7 looks at equal opportunities, drawing together themes from each element of the HRM cycle. The chapter focuses mainly on women, although much of what we say, particularly on employer policies, also applies to other groups such as ethnic minorities, older workers and people with disabilities. We argue that if organizations are to meet the challenges of the 1990s and beyond, they will have to make full use of the managerial potential of all groups, not just white, middle class males.

The concluding chapter draws together some of the key themes of the book, and summarizes the challenges that will face managers and those who manage them in the coming years.

Throughout the book, we have used 'boxes' to illustrate or expand upon points made in the text. Some boxes contain tables and diagrams; some present summaries of research findings; others consist of short case studies, or summaries of specific issues or debates. In all cases, the aim is to provide additional information or examples, without cluttering the main text unnecessarily. We believe that this approach makes for a more lively and readable presentation.

A major theme of the book is that organizations must adopt a strategic approach to managing their human resources in general, and their managers in particular. As Walker puts it:

> The challenge of managing human resources is to ensure that all activities are focused on business needs. All human resource activities should fit together as a system and be aligned with human resource strategies. These strategies, in turn, should be aligned with business strategies. (1992: 2)

According to this view, managing human resources is about achieving fit. There should be fit between the approach to managing people and the organization's objectives, whilst the various practices within the HRM cycle itself should also fit together as a coherent whole. For example, if the organization is committed to a strategy of differentiating itself from its competitors on the basis of high quality customer service, the appropriate HR strategies will underpin this, perhaps by providing training on customer service skills, by recruiting and developing quality staff, and by avoiding purely output-based pay systems. Box 1.4 develops the theme of matching HRM to corporate strategy in greater detail.

The idea of strategic fit suggests that whilst many organizations may face similar challenges, as outlined above, there is not necessarily one 'best way' to manage managers. The notion of strategic fit involves organizations matching their approach to HRM to their particular circumstances and strategies. Whilst we aim to provide a guide to research and best practice, and whilst each of the main chapters ends with a set of prescriptive guidelines, these cannot be reduced to simple, universally applicable checklists. The world is too complex a place for that.

Finally, our only reservation about the above statement from Walker is that it refers only to 'business'. It is our view that such arguments apply equally to public sector organizations, and perhaps even to some in the voluntary sector. As we shall see, organizations

Box 1.4 Matching organizational structure and HRM to strategy

Miles and Snow (1978) illustrate the way in which an organization's HR strategy relates to its environment and corporate strategy. They classify organizations into four strategic types: defenders, prospectors, analysers and reactors.

Defenders produce a limited product range aimed at a specific market niche, which they seek to dominate through cost efficiency. The emphasis is on stability and efficiency rather than on responsiveness to the market. The key HRM priority is the retention of career-minded individuals, through long-term development, seniority-based promotion and equitable rewards. People are recruited early in their career and steadily acquire the skills needed as they move up the promotional ladder.

Prospectors continually seek and exploit new opportunities, often moving on as competition increases. This degree of flexibility and speed of response demands an informal, decentralized structure. The key HRM priority is to recruit high-performing specialists as and when required, and the emphasis is on rewarding individual contribution, rather than long service.

Analysers move into new products or ventures only when they have been proven by others. They are likely to retain a core of traditional activities, and may well develop around this core. They need a degree of stability and formality to maintain the steady progression of the organization, but they also value innovation and enterprise, particularly in some parts of the organization. Analysers tend to recruit and develop inventive people early in their careers, and considerable resources are committed to training and development. This results in varied career paths for individuals, and the aim is to develop highly skilled managers who will remain loyal and be stimulated by job moves.

The fourth type, unlike the other three, represents those organizations which have not successfully matched their structure to their strategy. *Reactors* suffer poor performance because they respond inappropriately and inconsistently to market changes and have inappropriate structures. Reactors have no consistent policy, but attempt to recruit experts to solve immediate problems. There is often an emphasis on retrenchment rather than recruitment, promotion opportunities are scarce, and training and development are limited due to the scarcity of resources.

The above suggests that organizations need to match their HR strategies to corporate strategies. However, we live in a dynamic world. We have seen how environmental change is forcing many organizations to reassess their corporate strategies and structures.

Recent years have seen a clear move away from the defender

category, as increased competition and deregulation mean that fewer organizations have entrenched market positions, defendable on the basis of economies of scale and cost efficiency. Many such organizations have attempted a shift towards the analyser strategy, cautiously redefining their product base in line with customer requirements. There is still a need for stable HR systems, but there must be greater emphasis on individual performance and enterprise, at the expense of seniority and job security. HR strategies must be adapted to underpin this shift.

Other organizations have attempted to move from the defender to the prospector strategy. Here, the implications for HR are, if anything, more severe, with a shift towards the recruitment of specialists from the external labour market rather than through internal development.

Thus, many of the innovations in HRM in recent years can be traced to developments in corporate strategy, as organizations seek to come to terms with a changing environment. Of course, successful implementation of the appropriate HR strategies is not easy, as organizational cultures are often resistant to change. Many organizations have failed to make the transformation and have slipped into the reactor category, with all that that implies for long-term performance (Herriot and Pinder 1992).

in all sectors are increasingly recognizing the need for HRM to contribute towards the achievement of strategic goals.

Postscript: Who is a manager?

It will be useful to define at the outset what we mean by a manager. One possibility would be to define a 'manager' in terms of the precise functions carried out by those occupying the managerial role. However, whilst we discuss the managerial role below, we have opted instead for what Hales (1986: 89) calls a 'nominalist' approach, by taking as managers all those who would normally be referred to by that title. We use the term 'manager' to refer to all those in the organizational hierarchy above the level of first-line supervisor. We include in this definition those specialists who, whilst not necessarily directly responsible for the control of subordinates, nevertheless are of comparable status to line managers and are treated as such by the employer. Our definition thus includes such people as marketing and personnel managers, accountants and engineers, as well as line managers.

Management jobs are diverse, the mix of tasks and responsibilities depending on the function, the level in the hierarchy, and on the nature of the organization and its environment. However, there are a number of common themes, which have been summarized in the literature on the nature of managerial work (for example, Stewart 1976, 1982; Hales 1986; Dopson and Stewart 1990).

Managerial work tends to be unprogrammed and disjointed, with many short face-to-face encounters with subordinates and colleagues. Much of the manager's time is spent in communicating with others, rather than in quiet contemplation, and interruption is common, with subordinates often initiating the contact. Many managerial jobs are relatively loosely defined, leaving scope for the individual to determine the precise content and approach. Finally, managers are often caught between competing expectations – for example, those of superiors and subordinates, and of internal departments and external customers and suppliers. Managers typically have considerable discretion in their approach to the job, whilst the managerial role may be an ambiguous one. All this suggests that managerial jobs have the potential to be very satisfying, but at the same time to be highly stressful.

2
The Recruitment and Selection of Managers

The manager is a crucial figure in the success or failure of an organization, and finding and obtaining the best managers available is an issue of strategic importance. The recruitment and selection of managers is a complex, time consuming and expensive process. Making the wrong decisions, however, can be even more costly.

Organizations report recruitment and retention difficulties for managerial staff at all stages of the business cycle, and even during the recession of the early 1990s competition for the best managers remained keen. Those organizations failing to adopt professional and effective 'candidate-friendly' recruitment and selection practices will be less likely to attract the quality of managerial talent they need, with all that this implies for organizational performance (Herriot and Fletcher 1990).

In recent years, there has been considerable innovation in the recruitment and selection of managers. Some employers have attempted to deal with recruitment difficulties by enhancing their image with potential recruits. Some of the more sophisticated personnel departments have borrowed the ideas and approaches of their marketing colleagues in attempts to develop a 'brand image' for the organization, seeing recruitment as essentially 'job marketing'. A good example is provided by Stoy Hayward, who in an attempt to change graduate perceptions of accountancy produced an 'action-packed pulp novel' entitled *Never Say Boring Again!*

However, organizations have often failed to give sufficient attention to the hiring of managers. This chapter examines the key issues involved in managerial recruitment and selection. After an overview of the recruitment and selection process, we examine the main recruitment channels and selection methods used, paying particular attention to recent developments in employer practice.

Recruitment and selection

While there is much research on the selection practices of organizations, the recruitment phase has largely been ignored by researchers, and to some extent even by consultants (Smith et al. 1989). However, recruitment is crucial to the hiring process and it can be critical in securing cost-effectiveness.

Why is there such a preoccupation with the selection stage? It may reflect the priorities of occupational psychologists, who have concentrated their efforts on selection. It also reflects a tendency to see recruitment and selection as distinct and largely unrelated phases of staff hiring. In fact, the two phases are closely related. Under a recruitment-emphasized strategy, if a high calibre pool can be attracted in the first place, the selection decision becomes more difficult, but is perhaps less important. The reverse would also hold true.

We would argue that the most cost-effective strategy for hiring managers is one of good recruitment and good selection. To what extent does the recruitment and selection of managers measure up to this ideal in practice?

Recruiting managers: Recruitment channels

Box 2.1 summarizes the evidence on the use of recruitment channels for managers in the UK. Mackay and Torrington (1986) found that the majority of managers are recruited internally. The main external channel used is advertising, with national and professional media used most frequently. Local advertising for managers is used much less, but still more frequently than any of the other external channels. Consultants, Professional and Executive Recruitment (PER) and Executive Search are the other main channels used.

Other studies have found external advertising to be the most frequently used channel for recruiting managers. Large-scale surveys of *Guardian* readers, consisting mainly of '25–44 year old managers, professionals and executives', found a majority of respondents obtained their present posts through a recruitment advertisement (Beaumont 1989).

Although it refers to recruitment in general, and does not examine managerial recruitment in particular, the Institute of Personnel

Box 2.1 The recruitment of managers in the UK

Recruitment channel	Percentage of organizations using various recruitment channels			
	All managers (a)	General managers (b)	All managers (c)	All staff (d)
Advertising in national newspapers	–	53	59	78
Advertising in local newspapers	–	51	37	87
Advertising in all newspapers	48	–	–	–
Advertising in trade journals	21	24	68	80
Internal advertising	81	–	61	–
PER/Employment department	2	18	26	71
Selection consultants	16	21	31	61
Executive search	5	11	23	36
Personal contact	9	25	11	–
Number of organizations	701	239	350	1000

Sources: (a) Kingston 1971; (b) Gill 1980; (c) Mackay and Torrington 1986; (d) Curnow 1989.
'–' means not included in the particular survey questionnaire.

Management survey of over a thousand personnel managers contains evidence on changes in the use of recruitment channels (Curnow 1989). The survey found that recruiters in the late 1980s were making greater use of all advertising media and generally becoming more aggressive in their recruitment strategies. For example, there was an increasing use of the more outgoing forms of recruitment such as career conventions, open days, recruitment fairs and employer visits to universities (the so-called 'milkround').

Given the importance of press advertising and search and selection consultants, we examine these in more detail below. Internal recruitment is discussed further in chapter 5 where we review managerial careers.

Recruitment advertising

The volume of recruitment advertising has grown substantially since the 1950s, when national recruitment advertising was dominated by one newspaper carrying on average only six columns (Fordham 1983). As late as 1957, *The Times* refused to accept display advertising for jobs, but by the 1980s was offering free champagne to attract job advertisers (Watson 1989).

However, the pattern of expenditure on recruitment advertising is very volatile in the short term. For example, the total size of the recruitment advertising market for 1989 was around £650 million (Advertising Association 1990), whilst the recruitment consultants Austin Knight estimated that the market had declined to £450 million by 1991 (Schofield 1992).

Individual companies, such as British Airways, have substantial recruitment advertising expenditures, in excess of £1 million per year. However, this is dwarfed by spending on corporate advertising, with British Airways spending some £40 million in 1989 (Wyche 1990). Some organizations are now attempting to obtain synergy between recruitment and corporate advertising. Particularly prominent in this are the award winning recruitment advertisements of Apple and Ford which contain messages about new products, new technologies and product performance.

Recruitment advertising can be placed in a range of media, with a broad distinction being made between national, local and technical/trade/professional media. Their effectiveness as a source of managerial candidates can vary considerably. It appears that local media are little used by managerial job seekers, although they are relatively widely used by employers. This suggests that the targeting of advertisements for managers could be carried out more effectively. However, data on which to base an analysis of the effectiveness of recruitment advertising are extremely limited, with few organizations performing any form of response analysis despite being urged to do so by the textbooks.

Recruitment advertisements have received a great deal of criticism in recent years, both in terms of the design of advertisements and the effective choice of advertising media (Martin 1987; Barrow 1990; Resnick 1991). Although the design of recruitment advertisements is often seen as more of an art than a science, and does not reduce easily to a mechanical set of rules, there are some common pitfalls which the recruiter should be aware of. These include advertisements with:

- an emphasis on form rather than content, with flashy visuals and catchy headlines;
- overly complex language;
- language or visuals which may be taken to imply an intention to discriminate;
- a lack of detail on the post and on the organization;
- vague or non-existent salary specification, such as 'salary commensurate with experience', 'attractive salary', 'negotiable salary';
- a lack of prominence of the key details of the post: many managers read advertisements out of general interest and to check that they are receiving the going rate; such 'browsing' readers are attracted by a prominent display of salary, location, job title and company name;
- insufficient or vague details on the personnel specification sought, so that potential applicants are unable to effectively self-screen;
- odd requirements, as in the advertisement for a product manager who had to have a golf handicap of no greater than 18!
- ambiguous or vague instructions on how to apply for the post;
- onerous reply requirements, rather than simple requests for CVs and offers of information packs: for example, public sector posts (especially university posts) may ask the applicant to provide multiple copies of application forms and CVs. We recently noticed a request for 20 copies!

The construction of an effective advertisement which screens out unsuitable applicants and yet attracts the desired candidates is not easy. Schofield (1981) has suggested that to produce a successful advertisement the skills of the personnel manager need to be supplemented by those of the labour market expert, the professional copy writer, visualizer, finishing artist, typographer, media expert, production executive, administrator and finally the statistician. Such specialist skills are rarely all available in a single department, let alone a single individual.

The task is not made any easier by the behaviour of those applicants who do not meet the requirements profile but who still apply. A survey of over a thousand managers found that three-quarters would still apply even if they did not meet the specified requirements (City Research Associates 1988). The survey also suggests that there are other challenges facing the designer of recruitment adverts for managers; for example, over 30 per cent of managers did not know what 'circa' means when applied to an advertised salary!

What do managers themselves look for in a recruitment advertisement? The above survey suggests that managers want to be able to identify quickly the type of job being advertised. They do not tend to read those advertisements with catchy or cryptic headlines any more frequently than other advertisements. Indeed, they may be suspicious of such advertisements, and prefer full descriptions of the job, company and personnel specification. A large majority of managers felt it important that salary was shown, with 64 per cent saying that its absence would make them less likely to apply. Further, it appears that managers use the salary in a recruitment advertisement in deciding whether to read the advertisement in full or to move on to the next one.

Other surveys (for example, Guardian 1988; see box 2.2) support these findings and suggest that managerial and professional employees are becoming more demanding in their information requirements. In particular, managers say that they are reluctant to apply to organizations that appear 'faceless', as information on the nature of the organization is considered to be important by the potential applicant.

Box 2.2 What managers want in a recruitment advertisement

When asked: 'How important is it to you that recruitment advertisements give details of the following?', managers and professionals replied that the features below must always appear.

Feature	Percentage of managers saying feature must always appear
Place of work	92
Closing date for application	87
Salary	87
How to apply	86
Relevant experience required	85
Qualifications required	84
Job title	83
Duties	81
Responsibility	76
The company	69
Personal qualities required	67
Prospects	45
Age bracket suitable	39

Relocation expenses	38
Holiday/hours	25
Fringe benefits	25
Company car	24
Equipment/technology in use	22

Further analysis of the survey data showed that women were more concerned than men about holidays and hours of work and about the personal qualities specified in the advertisement, but were less concerned than men about fringe benefits.

Interestingly, the younger and older managers were more concerned than were those in the middle-age categories that details on age brackets should appear. Such applicants tend to be those at greatest risk of age discrimination for managerial posts and the inclusion of such information may be seen as helping to avoid wasting time in fruitless applications. Note, however, that the inclusion of age limits runs counter to current thinking on equal opportunities. Indeed, UK employers are being urged by government and other agencies to eliminate age discrimination, whilst in countries such as the USA and Australia, age discrimination is outlawed.

Younger people were also much keener to know more about career prospects, with 61 per cent of under-25s specifying this.

Source: Why Work? (*Guardian* 1988). Based on a sample of 25,973 managers and professionals.

When recruitment advertisements are examined against these preferences, there are some discrepancies. Content analysis of 3000 managerial recruitment advertisements by Redman and Mathews (1991, 1992a) found that many organizations are likely to appear 'faceless' to the managerial applicant, with nearly a third giving no details about the nature of the organization, and 5 per cent not even specifying where the organization is located. Details on the post to be filled and the personnel specification were also sketchy, while some 14 per cent did not specify salary. Perhaps most damning of all was that only 58 per cent of advertisements provided clear and unambiguous instructions on how to apply.

On all these criteria, the public sector does rather better than the private sector. This may reflect the fact that public-sector employers tend to be larger, and are more likely to have their own personnel specialists. Also, more of the public-sector advertising is designed in-house rather than through agencies, who emphasize 'creativity', often at the expense of basic details (Redman and Mathews 1992b). It may also reflect the influence of the National Association of Public Service Advertisers (NAPSA), set up in 1984, in the midst of escalating costs and growing recruitment difficulties, with the objective of improving public-service advertising.

Executive recruitment consultants

Many different types of organization are active in the executive recruitment industry. Public-sector organizations have been involved. PER was the largest and most well known of these and since its privatization in 1988 it has continued to be an important channel, particularly for younger and more junior staff. The Public Appointments Unit acts as the 'government's headhunter' (Clark 1989: 19), maintaining a list of people suitable for and interested in senior public ›
appointment. Professional institutes have also been involved; for example, the Institute of Chartered Accountants in England and Wales and the Institute of Chartered Surveyors have recruitment divisions.

However, the two main types of player in the executive recruitment industry are search consultants and selection consultants. Both offer a service to organizations. They differ, however, in the methods employed. The distinctive approach of search consultants is to seek potential candidates through direct personal contact, hence the colloquial term 'headhunters'. Selection consultants, on the other hand, identify potential applicants using open advertisements.

Distinguishing between search and selection consultants is further complicated, since many executive recruitment firms offer both of these services. However, specific assignments rarely combine the two, the personnel involved are often distinct, and they are marketed to and perceived by the users as distinct services (Clark 1989). We now examine both search and selection consultants.

Executive search   Executive search evolved in the USA as a recruitment method suitable for a vast country which had no single or comprehensive recruitment media coverage. In the UK, search has been used mainly in the recruitment of chief executives or directors. A survey of 150 companies found that one in five senior manager posts were filled in this way, with Finance Director, Marketing/Sales Director and Chief Executive the most common vacancies for which search consultants are used (Ian Ashworth and Associates 1988).

Box 2.3 Attracting managers via life themes

A recent development geared to the attraction of talented managers is the design of recruitment advertisements using 'theme theory'. A theme is a recurrent pattern of thought, feeling and behaviour, which is identified through focus-group discussions with outstanding performers in a particular occupation. A life theme is thus a conceptual organizing device, which can assist in the design of advertisements by drawing attention to those personal attributes which are linked to job success.

Life themes of productive sales professionals include competitiveness, empathy, work orientation, and stamina. Advertisements use life theme questions in an attempt to move people to apply for the post by appealing to specific individual attributes.

Life theme advertisements have been used by Joshua Tetley and Volvo. For example, in the advertisements for Volvo Business Sales Consultants the following were some of the life theme questions used:

- Are you a natural negotiator with a flair for getting the numbers right? (Persuasion and performance-orientation themes.)
- Do you have a strong need for independence in your work? (Ego-drive theme.)
- Can you develop and implement a sales strategy to achieve stretching targets? (Concept and focus themes.)
- Have you an outstanding ability to build good relationships and move senior people to a commitment? (Interpersonal and courage themes.)

Recruitment advertisements using life themes are claimed to have many benefits by SRI, the consultancy group most prominent in promoting their use in the UK. They are said to result in improved response quality; Joshua Tetley had a 1:6 ratio of candidates with good potential, a considerable improvement on their standard advertisements (Lunn 1987). Cost-effectiveness and increased shelf-life of recruitment campaigns are other claimed advantages.

The technique may even be seen as posing a threat to the recruitment advertising industry since, contrary to the conventional wisdom about advertising, the responses to a life theme advertisement appear not to diminish with repeated use.

Source: Hill and Maycock 1991.

Search has even been used for the recruitment of senior positions in trade unions; for example, the British Air Line Pilots' Association (BALPA) retained a headhunter to fill the post of General Secretary.

A survey of *The Times* Top 100 UK companies suggests that the two main reasons for using search are that it is perceived as producing the required candidates and that it provides a high degree of confidentiality (Clark and Clark 1990). Another survey suggested that most companies still prefer the more traditional recruitment methods, but that search consultants are often used when conventional advertisements have failed (Ian Ashworth and Associates 1988).

Executive search is a proactive recruitment strategy. The organization, via the headhunter, contacts the manager rather than vice versa as in other recruitment methods. Search consultants argue that job advertisements for middle and senior managers reach only those who are active job seekers and that these tend to be dissatisfied job holders or unemployed managers, so that the chances are against this producing the ideal person for a senior job (Trelawney 1981). Chalkey suggests that 'one has to find a man [sic] so wrapped up in his work that he rarely reads a newspaper' (1981: 29).

The headhunter's mode of operation is as follows. First, the consultant establishes the requirements of the post to be filled, drawing up a detailed job and person specification and constructing a search plan, culminating in a list of the most suitable candidates. Next, the headhunter approaches the potential candidates to sound out their interest, before compiling a short-list, with in-depth appraisals on each candidate derived from interviews. The search element is the most labour intensive part of the process and that most enshrined in mystery.

Headhunting is frequently and widely criticized. The most common criticisms are that headhunters are unethical, expensive, slow, fail to understand company needs, recommend unsuitable candidates and fail to keep the client sufficiently informed of progress (Adshead 1990). *Personnel Executive* described them as having:

> a collective image somewhere between the spy and the private detective: they were perceived as lurking furtively about in the half shadows of corporate management, only occasionally leaping out to snatch the best executive for someone else's use. (Anon 1981: 28)

Our interviews with personnel managers supported this critical view of headhunters. They were variously described as 'necessary evils', 'parasites' and 'hangers on'. One personnel manager of a large multinational chemical company described what he felt was a particularly unethical practice. A headhunter, who had recruited the organization's chief finance manager for a main competitor, approached the personnel manager with a 'you don't know you need me yet but . . .' introduction. Another strong criticism was that of the payment method for the headhunter's services, a third 'up front' on the retention of their services, a third on production of a short-list, and a third on appointment. Thus, organizations could spend a considerable amount of money before being sure of the quality of the service offered. Search consultants fees are sizeable, usually around a third of the manager's annual salary.

One study claims that consultants were often more concerned with keeping on the right side of the potential candidates than with putting them through a rigorous selection process, using selection techniques of low validity and reliability, such as unstructured interviews and references, rather than psychological testing (Clark 1989). However, many employers themselves can also be accused of relying mainly on such selection techniques (see box 2.6, below). Furthermore, not all the studies of the search industry have been damning, with a European survey rating the UK search industry as the best in Europe in terms of integrity (Rock 1990), and another survey finding only a small number of clients reporting major problems (Industrial Relations Services 1991b).

Perhaps it is not surprising that the search industry has taken its first tentative steps towards self-regulation by setting up the British Association of Executive Consultants (BAEC). The association had some fifteen founder members in 1990 and intends to restrict membership to 'senior-search' firms only. One of BAEC's first tasks is to develop a code of practice and to set standards in the level of service to be expected by users of executive search. The Institute of Personnel Management (IPM) is also attempting to regulate those consultants who are IPM members through the introduction of a code of conduct.

One danger in the use of headhunters is the potential for unfair discrimination. Access to senior positions by women and ethnic minorities may be hampered by headhunting, given its closed and 'clubbish' nature. Concern about the breach of equal opportunity principles is one reason why public sector organizations make less use of search consultants (Industrial Relations Services 1991b).

Despite their unpopularity, headhunters are here to stay – partly because they fill an organizational need, and perhaps because they confer added status on the headhunted managers, who can claim to be of such a rare calibre that they needed to be sought out individually.

Executive selection   Selection consultants sell their services by offering three main areas of expertise; in recruitment advertising, in selection skills, and in detailed and up to date knowledge of specific labour markets. All or some of these may be in short supply in the client organization, or the organization may simply not be able to devote in-house personnel staff to time-consuming executive recruitment. One Human Resource Director we interviewed described his company's use of selection consultants thus:

> Selection consultants double your resources, double your strength.
> They might not be as good as your guys, but you've got another body
> on board. And if you don't like him you can fire him. Dead easy.

Selection consultants also have the added advantage that advertisements can be placed anonymously, so that the client can maintain confidentiality in situations where it does not want to alert competitors to new developments or areas of weakness. (Although note our earlier comments on the advisability of identifying the organization in the advertisement.)

There is some debate between search and selection consultants as to the relative merits of the two approaches. Many companies automatically use search for posts over a specified salary level (Clark 1989). This appears to derive from a view, vigorously challenged by the selection consultants, that high-calibre senior managers will not respond to recruitment advertisements. However, selection consultants such as Price Waterhouse Executive Selection and Deloitte, Haskins and Sells, claim to achieve excellent results from advertisements, in terms of both quantity and quality of candidates. Advertising for senior positions rather than headhunting may also improve morale among existing staff, by suggesting that recruitment into the top jobs is open and meritocratic.

With no systematic research to support any of these claims it is difficult to draw any firm conclusions on the relative merits of search versus selection. Each has a number of particular advantages and disadvantages, and both are considerably more expensive than direct advertising.

Selecting managers

The adoption of a systematic, scientific, and professional approach to staff selection may pay dividends in terms of competitive advantage and bottom-line improvements. It may also help maintain corporate ethics (Bishop 1989). Interest in managerial selection has grown recently because organizations are increasingly concerned about the 'devastating effect of employing the wrong people, especially in senior positions' (Partridge 1990: 22).

One of Price Waterhouse's Canadian corporate clients estimated the potential benefits of a more sophisticated approach in the selection of an international tax planning manager. The client conservatively estimated the amount that both the 'highly competent' and 'average' manager would save the corporation in each of the first three years. The net present value of estimated tax savings for the 'average' manager was $3.5 million, compared to the 'highly competent' manager at $7.0 million (Van Clieaf 1991). An investment in selection technology that could differentiate between the two would certainly be cost-effective and would yield a good return on investment.

Many suggest that the selection and development of the managerial team is the key task of senior executives. Bishop (1989) has urged chief executives to take an active hands-on part in the selection of their top 150 managers. Others recommend that organizations should allow employees to participate in the selection of their managers, so that they feel more committed to them personally and actively involved in the management of their organization (Newstrom et al. 1987).

Whatever the merits of these views, one issue stands out as relatively uncontroversial:

> if success in managerial work depends upon the possession of a range
> of social skills and innate personal qualities, more attention needs to
> be paid to selection in order to guarantee the appropriate raw material.
> (Sisson and Storey 1988: 5)

Given this emphasis on the critical nature of management selection, it is perhaps surprising that so many organizations fail to give it a high priority. Anderson and Shackleton suggest that many managers view selection as a 'headache', as 'time consuming, costly, and an unwanted interruption of critical business activities' (1990: 5). Campbell-Johnston (1983) has even argued that the selection of managers is subject to a paradox, with a decreasing reliance on formal, systematic assessment techniques the more senior the management post. It may be that this is due to senior managers' unwillingness to allow a major role to their personnel specialists in the selection of senior staff.

Theory and practice in managerial selection

A selection technique can be assessed in terms of its reliability and validity. (This is true of any psychological technique; see for example chapter 3 on appraisal.) *Reliability* means that the technique should be consistent in the results it provides and not be unduly influenced by chance factors. For example, to what extent would a particular selection interviewer make the same judgements about a group of candidates if they interviewed them twice? This is referred to as intra-rater reliability. Also, to what extent would different interviewers agree on the assessment of a group of candidates? This is known as inter-rater reliability.

Validity refers to the extent to which the method actually measures the characteristic or ability it is supposed to. In the case of selection interviews, this would refer to the extent that they identify the 'good' candidates and reject the 'bad' candidates in terms of the characteristics being sought for the job.

Much of the theory and research on selection concerns itself with the technical soundness of particular techniques in terms of these criteria, and there is a great deal of advice available to the practitioner from psychologists and consultants. However, many managers complain that new concepts, theories, and techniques do not transfer easily from lecture room to board-room, and a number of studies have pointed to a major gap between theory and practice (see, for example, Bevan and Fryatt 1988; Knights and Raffo 1990).

Part of the reason for this gap is that those responsible for selection tend to select not on the basis of systematically defined job requirements, but in terms of ill-defined traits and attitudes (Robertson and Makin 1986: 52), or the alleged personality 'fit' between candidate and selector (Knights and Raffo 1990). Several studies confirm this emphasis on the candidate's personal attributes (Redman and Mathews 1991, 1992a; see box 2.4), and even in some cases those of the spouse (Campbell-Johnston 1983, see box 2.5). Thus, managerial selection is often more of a social than a technical process, reducing to the search for a 'good chap' (perhaps literally), with the main

Box 2.4 What do we want in a manager?

Content analysis of recruitment advertising for personnel and marketing managers reveals a wide range of personal attributes being requested. We found requests for fun-loving personnel managers and aggressive and streetwise product managers.

Here are the things which, according to the job advertisements, employers say they want:

administrative	flexible	personality
aggressive	friendly	persuasion
ambitious	fun-loving	political sensitivity
analytical	get-things-done	positive
approachable	go-getting	pragmatic
articulate	gregarious	presence
assertive	honest	presentation
behavioural skills	humorous	proactive
bright	imaginative	problem-solving
business awareness	independent	progressive
charismatic	influential	resilient
cooperative	initiative	resourceful
communication	innovative	results-orientated
conceptual	integrity	self-sufficient
confident	interpersonal skills	sensitive
creative	leadership	strategic thinker
credible	logical	streetwise
decisive	make-it-happen	strength-of-character
determined	management	tact
diplomatic	mature	team worker
drive	modern	tenacious
dynamic	motivated	tolerant
empathy	motivational	tough
enquiring	negotiation	thoughtful
enterprising	organization	versatile
enthusiastic	people	vision
flair		

Job advertisements often focus on personal characteristics rather than on achievements. We wonder how an employer would assess whether a candidate was indeed 'fun loving'. We have yet to hear of an interview panel asking candidates to tell their best three jokes!

Some employers seem to want everything. In one advertisement alone, 16 different qualities were specified. At times these appear to be contradictory; one advertisement called for 'an individualistic approach combined with the ability to fit in with a team'.

Source: Redman and Mathews 1991, 1992a.

Box 2.5   Trial by luncheon

A common approach is to informally observe the candidate in a social situation, usually during a meal or casual drinks.

I believe every serious candidate should be taken out to lunch or dinner to observe at first hand his [sic] behaviour and conduct in a public setting. I recall a search we conducted for a company president of a well known manufacturer. We flew a promising candidate in for luncheon with the key people involved at the company and went to a popular buffet-style restaurant. After we were seated, we got up and walked over to the buffet table to get our food. Everyone in our party could only watch in shock as this candidate eliminated himself from contention without ever uttering a word. The individual proceeded to load his plate with food to the point of people staring (to our great embarrassment). To make matters worse, some items that are traditionally forked or spooned onto a plate, this person hand-picked. After sitting down, his dining manners proved to be as poor as the lack of social grace displayed at the buffet table. (Bishop 1989: 24)

Such social situations may also provide an opportunity to 'interview' the prospective candidate's spouse.

There is considerable benefit to be gained from taking the prospective candidate and his or her spouse out to dinner. You will be able to assess how far the spouse will be a good ambassador for your company in the way he or she supports the candidate. (Campbell-Johnston 1983: 328)

Such approaches emphasize the social rather than the technical nature of managerial selection, the search for 'one of us', and must raise a number of serious questions. Not least is the questionable reliability and validity of such processes, along with the danger of implicit discrimination on social, gender and racial grounds.

selection criteria being acceptability rather than suitability in terms of specific competencies or qualifications.

This emphasis on informality in selection may reflect the preferences of line managers (Knights and Raffo 1990). They may value informality and resist what they perceive as bureaucracy in the selection process. Many managers pride themselves on their innate ability to 'pick winners', and some claim that they can distinguish good candidates by their firm handshake or by looking them in the eye!

We interviewed a personnel manager at a medium-sized textile company, who described his lack of influence in the managerial selection process thus:

> I might as well not be there. All my attempts to introduce new selection techniques have got nowhere here. They never will while the current managing director is here. He thinks he has this wonderful ability to spot talent. But he doesn't have to sort the mess out when we have had to get rid of his mistakes. That's my job.

Line managers continue to hold sway over the selection process, not least because they are the 'breadwinners', and personnel departments often lack the status locally to challenge them. Some personnel managers themselves appear happy to go along with this informal approach to selection, rather than press for a more professional approach. This seems to be especially likely for those personnel managers who lack formal training and have moved into personnel roles from line management positions (Collinson 1991). Acquiescence to the line manager's preference for decisions based upon personal attributes also reflects a distinct lack of faith among personnel managers themselves in the accuracy of the more formal, systematic techniques advocated as part of the 'professional' approach to selection.

However, the explanation for the gap between theory and practice does not rest solely with the practitioner. The theoretical models used by occupational psychologists are often inadequate. For example, most selection models implicitly assume that managers' effectiveness is independent of the context in which they are required to manage, and yet evidence suggests that the success of managers is situationally specific (Kotter 1982).

Managerial selection in practice

The results of the major surveys on managerial selection in the UK are displayed in box 2.6. There is evidence of innovation in recent years. Not only have many employers experimented with testing or assessment centres for the first time, but those who previously used them appear to be using them more widely. A recent survey found that 62 per cent of employers using psychometric tests were using them more often, and employers have introduced new and more valid forms of standard techniques (Industrial Relations Services

Box 2.6   Managerial selection in practice: The survey evidence

Selection technique	Percentage of organizations using the technique to select managers				
	(a)	*(b)*	*(c)*	*(d)*	*(e)*
Interviews	92	99	96	91	100
References	–	96	76	85	96
Cognitive tests	9	29	12	65	70
Personality tests	8	36	19	64	64
Trainability tests	–	–	1	5	–
Graphology	1	8	–	–	3
Biodata	–	6	–	–	19
Assessment centres	–	21	–	–	59
Application form/CV	–	–	–	94	93
Number of organizations surveyed	281	108	350	318	73

Sources: (a) Gill 1980 (general managers); (b) Robertson and Makin 1986 (all managers); (c) Mackay and Torrington 1986 (all managers); (d) Bevan and Fryatt 1988 (managers and professionals); (e) Shackleton and Newell 1991 (all managers).

1991a). There is a danger of exaggerating the scale and effect of these developments, as we argue below, but since the early 1980s there has been a degree of innovation in managerial selection.

Why are more employers professionalizing their approach to managerial selection? Cost-effectiveness does not seem to have been a key consideration, and there appears to have been little progress towards rigorous cost-benefit evaluation of selection methods (Industrial Relations Services 1991a).

A key factor appears to have been recruitment and retention difficulties, especially apparent during the late 1980s, when organizations were being urged to adopt more 'candidate-friendly' selection methods (Herriot and Fletcher 1990). An organization which persisted with unsophisticated selection processes would run the risk of being perceived as unprofessional and its attractiveness to candidates would suffer. In a sellers' market this would serve to exacerbate an already difficult recruitment situation.

Other reasons for innovation in selection techniques include increasing attention to equal opportunities (see chapter 7), changes in job content and work practices, the introduction of TQM and customer care programmes, and the appointment of new personnel specialists committed to greater professionalism in selection (Industrial Relations Services 1991a).

These developments begin to call into question the alleged gap between theory and practice (Anderson and Shackleton 1990). There is room for some cautious optimism with the increased use of testing and assessment centres, techniques which are generally regarded as more effective than more traditional methods (see box 2.7). Thus, the 'message of psychological research about reliability and validity of different selection methods is beginning to reach practitioners in the field' (Shackleton and Newell 1991: 34).

In the remainder of this chapter, we examine some of the main techniques used in the selection of managers.

Interviews

According to the surveys, most managers are selected by interviews. One survey found that 60 per cent of British companies and 92 per cent of French companies always used two or more interviews in their selection of managers (Shackleton and Newell 1991). This is in spite of the fact that occupational psychologists have criticized interviews for their lack of reliability and validity (Robertson and Makin 1986).

The most common type of interview used in the UK is that involving two or three selectors. Panel interviews involving four or more selectors appear to be something of a rarity, with most companies never using them. Only in parts of the public sector is the large panel interview common.

Management selection interviews are more usually conducted by line managers than by personnel specialists, the latter playing only a minor role in selection decisions even where they are involved (Knights and Raffo 1990). Personnel's main role appears to be one of 'servicing' line management, including pre-selection screening and the drawing up of short-lists, administering tests, following up references, and checking qualifications (Gill 1980; Mackay and Torrington 1986). In general, the manager's peers have little or no involvement in interviews or indeed in the wider selection process. This is perhaps surprising given the increasing emphasis on teamwork.

Box 2.7   Accuracy of selection methods

Managers cannot be selected with perfect accuracy, whatever technique is used. However, some techniques are more accurate than others at predicting future job performance.

The accuracy of any technique can be seen as the correlation between the selection assessment (such as a test score or an evaluation from an interview) and subsequent job performance (such as a measure of productivity or an appraiser's rating).

The correlation coefficient lies somewhere between plus and minus 1, with +1 showing perfect selection, 0 representing random selection, and a minus figure showing a negative correlation. As a general guideline, a coefficient greater than +0.3 would be seen as an acceptable level of accuracy.

Much research has been conducted on the accuracy of various selection techniques, using a variety of performance indicators. In the diagram, we present the consensus of opinion from a large number of such studies.

Correlation coefficient		*Accuracy of selection method*
1.0	—	Perfect prediction
0.9	—	
0.8	—	
0.7	—	Structured behaviour interview (0.70)
		Assessment centres (for promotion) (0.65)
0.6	—	
		Work sample tests (0.54); ability tests (0.53)
0.5	—	
		Assessment centres (for performance) (0.43)
0.4	—	Personality tests, modern (0.39); bio data (0.38)
0.3	—	Panel interview (0.37)
0.2	—	References (0.23); traditional one-on-one interview (0.20)
0.1	—	
0.0	—	Chance prediction; astrology; graphology
−0.1	—	

Sources: Smith 1988; Smith et al. 1989; Van Clieaf 1991.

When employers were asked why they used interviews, the most common response was to filter out unsuitable candidates. Some 47 per cent of organizations used the interview for predicting subsequent job performance and 39 per cent for predicting group compatibility (Bevan and Fryatt 1988). Despite the interview's many critics, the vast majority of respondents in the surveys say that they are content with the reliability of the interview as a selection instrument.

Given the enduring popularity of the interview, it is worth considering how it can be made more effective as a selection tool. Interviewers should certainly receive training in interview techniques and a systematic approach to defining job requirements is essential, not least for equal opportunities reasons (see chapter 7). Developments such as the 'behavioural event interview' are also worthy of consideration (see box 2.8). The key is to avoid an unstructured, overly subjective approach by basing the selection decision on job requirements as systematically as possible.

Testing

Organizations have been making increasing use of psychometric tests in management selection (Mabey 1989; Industrial Relations Services 1991a), and supporters of tests go so far as to suggest that there is no job for which a test cannot be found to predict performance.

There are many different types of psychometric tests used in the selection process. They can be classified according to what they aim to test: for example, intelligence, aptitude, knowledge, skill, personality, trainability, and honesty. They may also be classified according to how they are conducted: for example, task performance, paper and pencil, questionnaires, and group tests. The main categories of psychological measurement used for selecting managers are tests of aptitude and achievement, termed cognitive tests and personality tests.

Part of the attraction of using tests in selection stems from the wide range available, their relative ease of use and, of course, from the claim that they reduce the degree of subjectivity. Cognitive tests appear to be used mainly as part of a filtering or pre-selection process (Bevan and Fryatt 1988).

However, there is an air of mystique and the 'black arts' surrounding the use of psychometric tests. Bevan and Fryatt (1988) found that when questioned whether their tests were reliable or not as a predictor of job performance, around four-fifths of employers simply did not know.

Box 2.8 Recent developments in selection interviewing: The behavioural event interview

Behavioural event interviews (BEI) have been found to have one of the highest predictive validities compared to other selection techniques (see box 2.7). This high level of validity, coupled with the increasing interest in managerial competencies, has stimulated their use as a selection tool. Organizations such as ICI and Cadbury-Schweppes use BEIs as a central element of their hiring process.

ICI applied BEI in the production, R&D and commercial functions of its Chemicals and Polymers (C&P) division. The process began with a 'job competency analysis', carried out by the Boston-based consulting group, McBer. This involved in-depth interviews with 96 employees from the three functions, examining critical work-based incidents. The aim here was to interview better-performing employees, so as to identify what they do that makes them perform well.

Transcripts from these interviews were then read by an ICI team under the guidance of McBer, and an overview of the abilities and behaviours that had led to successful outcomes was formed. The interviewees were divided into sub-groups of 'superior' and 'competent' performers, based largely on organizational ratings, and a frequency count was made of the abilities and behaviours associated with each sub-group.

From this analysis, ICI identified three broad classes of competency:

- *Distinguishing competencies* These were held in common across the three functions and distinguished 'superior' and 'competent' performers from inferior performers.
- *Threshold competencies* Competencies held in common across the three functions which did not distinguish competent performers, but which functioned as minimum requirements of effective performance.
- *Functional competencies* Competencies which appeared to have special importance for particular functions.

These three classes of competence were put together to form an overall model for professional and managerial jobs in the C&P group, termed the Key Elements of Outstanding Performance.

Initially used for graduate recruitment, BEIs and the C&P competency model now form the basis for recruitment and promotion processes throughout the division, as well as impacting on other HRM processes such as career planning, performance appraisal, and training and development.

Source: Interviews with ICI managers.

In an analysis of the predictive ability of three of the most widely used personality tests – Cattell's 16 PF, the Californian Psychological Inventory and the Occupation Personality Questionnaire – Blinkhorn and Johnson (1990) found little evidence of a relationship between test scores and job performance. They suggest that personality tests are little more than 'bits of stage managed flummery intended to lend an air of scientific rigour to personnel practice' (Fletcher et al. 1991: 39). According to Blinkhorn their misplaced popularity with selectors derives from 'good marketing, wishful thinking, bad statistics' (1991: 3).

Others have leapt to the defence of personality tests and take issue with the Blinkhorn analysis. The strengths claimed for personality tests include their ability to predict a wide range of behaviour, helping the selector to structure interviews, and facilitating the selection of the most effective managerial team (Fletcher et al. 1991).

Several practical difficulties can arise with the use of tests. Firstly, the training provided for users of psychometric tests is often inadequate. Given that increasing numbers of organizations are using tests and the number of tests available on the market is growing, this issue is one of rising importance. This has led the British Psychological Society to produce, in conjunction with the Institute of Personnel Management, a certificate of competence in occupational testing.

Secondly, tests are often perceived as having an air of finality about them; the managerial applicant either passes or fails. In fact, such tests can provide a substantial amount of information about an applicant, which can form the basis for both the organization and the applicant to make decisions, provided that this is available in a form that can be easily digested by both. However, in practice candidates, and indeed managers responsible for selection decisions, may receive very little information about test results. In the Industrial Relations Services survey (1991a), 20 per cent of test users provided no feedback whatsoever to candidates, and of those that provided feedback, in 15 per cent of cases this was to the successful candidate only. Others provided it to unsuccessful candidates only on request. Where feedback is provided, it is often limited to a final score, and a '28' or '42' conveys little informational content.

Fletcher (1986) argues the case for full verbal feedback to candidates on test results, if only on the ethical grounds that it is the candidate who should own the data. Robertson and Makin (1986) have argued that the selection process in general is marked by a lack of sharing of information between applicant and selector, and that this is to the detriment of both parties. This is especially so with selection tests, which are demanding on the candidate in terms of both time and emotional involvement.

A final difficulty with tests is that they tend to be used in a piecemeal and *ad hoc* fashion. Tests are rarely integrated into the wider HRM practices for managers. One notable exception to this is at STC-ICL, part of the Fujitsu group (Jones 1990). The internal 'Investing in People' programme translates the company's polices, values and beliefs into a set of practical people-management processes. These are summarized in management handbooks, which set out what the line manager is responsible for and offer advice on how these responsibilities should be achieved, including the handling of psychometric testing.

Assessment centres and situational interviews

The assessment centre is a highly developed selection tool which, in contrast to the indirect nature of most other selection techniques, assesses individuals on the basis of their performance in a series of job-related tasks and problems (see chapter 5 for a fuller discussion of the technique). Assessment centres have been used by a growing number of large companies, particularly for graduate recruitment and also as part of management development programmes.

For selection purposes, a number of organizations have developed a shortened version, known as the 'situational interview', which is less time-consuming and more cost-effective than the full assessment centre (Gabris and Rock 1991). The situational interview is widely used in the USA (Maurier and Fay 1988; Gabris and Rock 1991) and is becoming increasingly popular in the UK. Rather than the assessment relying largely on inferences based on the candidate's past, candidates are presented with hypothetical situations based on the functions they would actually perform in the job and asked how they would respond. The questions are not informally derived hypothetical situations, but are based on a systematic job analysis, designed to determine the essential skills for the job.

For example, an insurance company used the following question to select school-leaver entrants for sales positions:

> You have called on a broker to keep an appointment arranged by telephone to discuss the progress of a sales campaign. His secretary tells you he is out of the office all day. As you are leaving, you bump

into the broker, together with a representative of another insurance company, coming out of another room. What would you do? (Quoted in Syrett 1988: 1)

Good performers would be expected to greet the person warmly, make another appointment, and remain dignified. Bad performers on the other hand would point out to the broker that they expected appointments to be kept, or challenge the broker with the secretary's false explanation.

Given the emphasis on the hypothetical rather than actual experience, the situational interview can be particularly useful in assessing the managerial potential of those who as yet have no management experience. For example, NatWest Bank has used situational interviews to assess staff for their suitability for entry to its management development programme.

Summary and conclusions

In this chapter, we have described some of the key developments in the recruitment and selection of managers. Despite its many critics, the interview is likely to retain its popularity. However, there has been some increase in the use of selection methods with greater validity and reliability, including assessment centres, testing, and more structured interviews. This is to be welcomed.

It may be that the adoption of new techniques has been driven by the recruitment and retention difficulties of the late 1980s, rather than by any overwhelming desire among employers to improve cost-effectiveness, fairness or professionalism. It will be interesting to see whether the trend towards greater sophistication continues into the longer term.

Given the substantial investment that managerial recruitment represents, and the high costs of making a poor decision, it is worth concluding the chapter with some basic guidelines for the recruiter.

- Do not neglect the recruitment phase. The attraction of a good field of candidates is a key part of the recruitment and selection process.
- Think of recruitment as 'job marketing' and give it the same kind of attention afforded to product or service marketing.
- Ensure that your choice of recruitment channels is well targeted at the particular management specialism you seek.
- Design recruitment efforts to encourage applicants to self-screen. This

helps contain costs. The use of advertisements based on life themes may be helpful in this respect.

- Consider the use of the more valid and reliable selection techniques, such as testing, structured interviews and assessment centres. This can improve cost-effectiveness if it results in fewer bad decisions.
- Consider involving a wider range of personnel in the selection process. With the emphasis now on building the managerial team, it may be appropriate to involve the manager's future peers.

Finally, recruiters should avoid sophistication for its own sake. Costs as well as benefits need to be taken into account, and recruitment and selection methods should be systematically monitored and evaluated.

Further reading

A guide to the theory and practice of selection, written with the practitioner in mind, is Mike Smith, Mike Gregg and Dick Andrews, *Selection and Assessment: A New Appraisal*, London: Pitman, 1989. A study of the state of selection in the UK is Stephen Bevan and Julie Fryatt, *Employee Selection in the UK*, Brighton: Institute of Manpower Studies, 1988.

3

Appraising Managerial Performance

Performance appraisal is a key tool in making the most of an organization's human resources. There is a simple reason for this: what gets measured, gets done. Performance appraisal is far too important to be left to an annual event, and should be an ongoing process. As Odiorne suggests: 'Nothing improves your driving like being followed by a police car' (1990: 38).

Barlow (1989) argues that managerial appraisal systems serve to reassure significant others, not least directors and shareholders, that economic rationality is being pursued. He suggests that management appraisal systems may signal to the outside world that the organization is acting in a 'proper manner'. Failure to use appraisal schemes would invite not only a questioning of organizational legitimacy but would also risk being seen as 'capricious, negligent, and irrational' (1989: 499).

It is no surprise then that appraisal for managerial employees is widespread. But how effective is it in practice? One study of the appraisal of middle managers found that appraisal interviews seldom lasted more than fifteen minutes and that those senior managers who acted as appraisers derived more information from third parties, usually in the form of complaints, than from direct interaction with the appraised manager (Finn and Fontaine 1983). Studies of performance appraisal for senior managers report similar concerns about effectiveness (Longenecker and Gioia 1988).

One manager in a recent study we conducted summed up the attitude to the managerial performance appraisal system in his organization:

The general attitude to performance appraisal is 'Oh my God, its appraisal time again. I suppose we had better do it.' But what the hell are we doing it for?

Most managers in large and medium-sized organizations are subject to formal appraisal, and with the increasing use of performance appraisal at lower levels in the organization they are often appraisers themselves. In this chapter, we consider the implications of these roles for the management of managers.

The origins of performance appraisal

Informal appraisal has been going on for as long as people have been working together. There is a basic human tendency to make judgements about our work colleagues. Formal performance appraisal, however, has a shorter history. George (1972) suggests that formal performance appraisal in industry originated in Scotland in the early 1800s with the 'silent monitor' used in Robert Owen's textile mills. A multi-coloured block of wood was hung over the employees' machines, with the front colour indicating the superintendent's assessment of the previous day's conduct, from white for excellent through yellow for good, blue for indifferent and black for bad. Given the complexity of some modern systems of performance appraisal, many managers may secretly yearn for such a simple and unambiguous system!

Much of the subsequent development of performance appraisal occurred in the USA. The general interest in appraisal was boosted by the influences firstly of 'scientific management', with its particular focus on the quantification of performance, and later by the work of the 'human relations' school and their examination of the more subjective influences on employee performance.

Why are managers appraised?

There are many reasons why managers are appraised. Randell (1989) summarizes the main purposes of performance appraisal as follows:

- Evaluation. To enable the organization to share out the rewards and promotions fairly.
- Auditing. To discover the work potential, present and future, of individuals and departments.
- Succession planning. To construct plans for human resource, departmental and corporate planning.

- Controlling. To ensure that employees meet organizational standards and objectives.
- Training. To discover learning needs.
- Development. To develop individuals by advice and information and to shape their behaviour by praise or punishment.
- Motivation. To add to employees' job satisfaction by understanding their needs.
- Validation. To check the effectiveness of personnel procedures and practices.

The above list suggests that we expect a lot of our appraisal systems. UK studies of performance appraisal in practice show that organizations use performance appraisal to assess training and development needs, review past and improve current performance, set performance objectives, assess promotion potential and determine salaries (see box 3.1). The objectives of performance appraisal in the USA seem to be even broader, with Fombrun and Laud (1983) reporting its use for termination, manpower planning and the validation of selection methods, in addition to the above. In recent years, there appears to be a shift away from using performance appraisal for the assessment of managerial potential and career planning, and an increase in its use for improving current performance (Gill 1977; Long 1986).

The use of performance appraisal for a range of objectives may help to integrate the various HRM practices, for example by providing a link between performance management and the identification of training and development needs. However, there is a problem with trying to achieve multiple objectives with a single appraisal system, in that the process may become confused, and the various objectives may conflict. For example, in a system that simultaneously attempts to make judgements about past, current and potential performance there is a danger that the appraiser may become confused between these three very different issues, so that the validity of the process is undermined.

It is usually argued that the nature of the appraisal process differs according to whether the main emphasis is on making judgements about a manager's performance or determining the manager's future development needs (see box 3.2). However, in practice, even the most developmental systems inevitably involve an element of judgement about current performance, so that there is usually at least some potential for conflict for appraisers between the roles of judge and counsellor.

Box 3.1 The uses of performance appraisal: Survey evidence

The UK

Function	Percentage of organizations		
	(a)	(b)	(c)
Assess training and development needs	96	81	97
Improve current performance	92	81	97
Review past performance	91	79	98
Assess future potential/promotability	87	76	71
Career planning	81	64	75
Set performance objectives	57	62	81
Assess salary	39	76	40
Others (e.g. updating personnel records)	–	3	4
Number of organizations surveyed	230	264	250

Sources: (a) Gill 1977; (b) Mackay and Torrington 1986; (c) Long 1986.

The USA

Function	Percentage of organizations
Merit increases	91
Job counselling/feedback	90
Promotion	82
Termination	64
Performance potential	62
Succession planning	57
Career planning	52
Transfer	50
Manpower planning	38
Bonuses	32
Development/evaluation of training programmes	29
Internal communication	25
Selection validation	16
Expense control	7
Number of organizations surveyed	256

Source: Fombrun and Laud 1983.

Box 3.2 Models of performance appraisal: Two ideal types

	Judgement orientated	*Development orientated*
Appraiser role	judge; measuring	counsellor; facilitating
Interview style	telling	discussing
Time perspective	past	future
Standards used	organization/superior's	self-assessed
Aim	control	personal growth

The use of performance-related pay awards based upon appraisal outcomes (see chapter 6) may give rise to particular problems. The appraisee's fear of losing a pay rise may limit the openness of the discussion. Performance problems may be explained away, attributed to others or blamed on bad luck, rather than forming the basis for a discussion of management development needs. Some organizations attempt to reduce this tension by paying merit increases some months after the appraisal. Others have separate appraisal and development interviews. However, it may be unrealistic to expect appraisers and appraisees to treat the two as distinct, since it is unlikely that the pay rise can be put completely out of mind.

Some studies of appraisal have found that potentially the most motivating aspect for the appraisee is the identification of individual training and development needs (see, for example, Alimo-Metcalfe 1992). However, in practice, appraisees often complain that this aspect of the process is neglected, with a lack of follow up once needs have been identified (Snape et al. 1993). Where this is so, organizations could be accused of failing to make the most of the appraisal process.

How are managers appraised?

It is not difficult to develop an appraisal system which looks good on paper. The real difficulties are more often encountered in trying to make a scheme work. Appraisers should be given a proper intro- duction to the scheme, along with training in objectives-setting, interviewing, listening skills and the provision of constructive feedback. However, in practice, such preparation is often very limited, and an appraisal scheme must be robust enough to survive not only inadequate introduction and limited appraiser training, but also indifferent levels of manager–subordinate communication, and the average interpersonal skills of the appraiser (Fletcher 1987).

Randell (1989) suggests that the nature of a performance appraisal system can tell us a great deal about how an organization views its staff. He argues that the format of an appraisal scheme is determined by senior managers' views on what factors influence work performance, rather than by specific objectives for the system. If senior managers believe that the past is the main determinant of the present and the future, the appraisal system will be based on an information-gathering and decision-making procedure and emphasize a comprehensive assessment of past strengths and weaknesses. Equally, if the 'pull' of future events is viewed as being the main influence on work performance, the appraisal system will concentrate on the work to be achieved, as the basis for reward and promotion opportunities.

There are many approaches to appraisal and those in most common use are summarized in box 3.3. These range from relatively simple techniques such as ranking and traits rating, to more complex and elaborate methods such as behaviourally anchored rating scales. The techniques also vary between those that emphasize the past, such as

---

Box 3.3 Appraisal methods

Alphabetical/ numerical	Assess performance against ratings criteria on a scale ranging from high to low performance, e.g. 1–5, A–F.
Trait rating scales	Assess performance against a list of personality traits.
Behaviourally anchored ratings scale (BAR)	Assess performance on a ratings scale anchored to specific descriptions of work behaviour.
Forced distribution ratings	Rating employees on scales with a fixed percentage of employees stipulated for each scale point or range of points.
Ranking	Rater lists the appraisees from best to worst, often using a single global performance trait.

Paired comparisons.	The rater compares every possible pair of individuals in a department, rating one as a superior performer, producing an overall ranking by summing across all paired comparisons.
Management by objectives/results-based	Setting of future objectives and action plans jointly between appraiser/appraisee and measuring subsequent performance against objectives. Systems vary in extent to which objectives are accompanied by agreed action plans.
Work Standards Approach (WSA)	Comparing actual performance against expected levels of performance.
Written report/narrative/essay	Written commentary describing strengths, weaknesses and achievements.
Critical incident method	Rater documents key positive and negative events that have occurred during given period. May be used as basis for written report.

rating and ranking techniques, and those that also focus on the future, such as management by objectives.

According to the surveys of managerial appraisal in practice, objectives-based approaches appear to dominate (box 3.4). Particularly at more senior levels, appraisal systems tend to rely less on homogeneous and standardized criteria and more on job-based, results-orientated and essentially individualized systems (Fombrun and Laud 1983).

Arguably, appraising performance on the basis of measurable objectives allows for greater objectivity than with appraisal based on, for example, personality traits or ranking, since the focus is on observable job performance, rather than on abstract, ill-defined or implicit criteria. In particular, there is perhaps less chance of appraisers being prone to 'halo' or 'horns' effects in their assessments.

However, the use of objectives-based appraisal systems is not without its problems. Since managerial goals are individualized under such systems, it may be particularly difficult to achieve equitable ratings. Furthermore, there is the danger that the managers' actions may account for little of the variability in the outcomes measured. Where this is so, it is likely to result in disillusionment with the

Box 3.4 How are managers appraised?

Figures refer to percentage of organizations using each method of managerial appraisal.

The UK

MBO/results	Alpha/ numerical	Written report	Traits	Self-rating	Other
44.4	24.8	50.4	5.6	14.3	7.9

Based upon all levels of managers (N = 268).
Source: Mackay and Torrington 1986.

The USA

Management level	Type of appraisal system				
	MBO*	Objectives*	Essay	WSA	BAR
Supervisory (N = 235)	37	38	36	32	25
Middle (N = 238)	44	42	37	27	24
Top (N = 217)	43	39	33	24	18
Professionals (N = 234)	39	36	36	33	24

*Survey defined 'MBO' as objectives-based with agreed action plans, whilst 'Objectives' defined as objectives-based but without explicit action plans.
Source: Fombrun and Laud 1983.

appraisal process and possible demotivation, especially if there is a link with rewards.

Another possible problem with objectives-based systems is that if the managers' targeted outcomes are not achieved, the appraiser may be unable to counsel on what the manager should do, should stop doing, or should do differently to get the outcomes back in line. The problem is not the emphasis on outcomes as such, but the neglect of job analysis to identify the critical behaviours which the individual manager has control over and which effect the outcome measures (Latham 1986).

Box 3.5   Competency-based appraisal at the National and Provincial Building Society

The UK's National and Provincial employs some 3500 staff working in over 400 different roles. The Society uses an assessment of an individual's competencies in the appraisal of all its employees, from director to part-time cashier. The competency model evolved from, and is designed to directly support, the mission and corporate strategy of the National and Provincial.

Various combinations and levels of 44 competencies are used. Each competency is specified in terms of behavioural outcomes and a competency profile for each job role is identified. The competencies are grouped into three categories: the employee's knowledge and capability, individual contribution, and team contribution.

The initial framework was based on 'key post competencies' collected during 1988–9, in part by getting staff to identify the skills they used on 'good days', and the skills that could have reduced the impact of 'bad days'. The scheme has evolved over time in response to staff feedback and changes in the external market. A major change resulting from staff feedback has been the expansion of the evaluation of the more technical skills areas of numeracy, accountancy and finance.

Following the assessment interview, the competency profile forms the basis for a personal development plan and the setting of individual performance objectives based upon business goals, personal development, and the National and Provincial's corporate 'values' of accountability, customer care, enterprise and success. This assessment also forms the basis for a performance-related pay award.

The system is monitored using a software package that is designed to identify suspected bias and to facilitate the wider use of the data for human resource planning.

Sources: Falconer 1991, and interviews with National and Provincial managers.

A number of organizations, including ICI and National and Provincial, have begun to tackle this latter issue by using job competencies as part of the appraisal criteria, often in conjunction with working objectives (see box 3.5). Job competencies are defined in terms of the observable skills and behaviours thought to be necessary for the performance of a particular job. Competencies are carefully defined, usually by interviewing those in close contact with the job, and various levels or degrees of competency are identified. Appraisers are then asked to assess individuals in terms of the extent to which they display the defined competencies, and an overall rating is derived from this. This approach differs from the old-fashioned traits approach in that competencies are more rigorously defined in terms of observable behaviour, and are derived from an analysis of specific job requirements.

Used in combination with working objectives, such an approach has the advantage not only of focusing on job outcomes, but of highlighting the behavioural changes necessary for improved performance. It can also allow organizations to identify those managers who are over-promoted, those who could be more effective, those who have reached the limit of their potential and those who should be treated as high-fliers (see chapter 5).

Who appraises managers?

The effectiveness of the appraisal process depends on the participants, the methods used, and the contextual factors surrounding it. A key factor within this is the choice of appraiser.

The choice of appraisers for managers is closely related to the decision on the method of appraisal, as the appraisers are in a sense the measuring instrument; they are the ones who fill out the forms, conduct the interviews, and define and interpret the measures. Oddly, perhaps, the performance appraisal literature is focused mainly on techniques and has given little attention to the context in which they are to be applied and even less to who applies them. Such an omission perhaps explains why the theory of performance appraisal is often studiously ignored in practice.

For the majority of managers in the UK, appraisal is still a 'top-down process', with most being appraised by their immediate superior (see box 3.6), although there has been some growth in the use of 'grandparent' managers as appraisers. Appraisal systems using multiple raters appear to be on the increase, if somewhat slowly. However, this is largely limited to the use of parent and grandparent managers, and none of the UK surveys reports the use of subordinates or customers as appraisers. Peer appraisal is used, via a management development committee, in only a small number of organizations. Survey evidence from the USA paints a similar picture,

Box 3.6 Who appraises managers?

Appraiser	Percentage of organizations		
	(a)	(b)	(c)
Immediate manager	86	93	79
Grandparent manager	12	12	40
Personnel department	–	5	10
Other (e.g. management development committee, assessment centre)	2	1	3
Number of organizations surveyed	230	250	271

Sources: (a) Gill 1977; (b) Long 1986; (c) Mackay and Torrington 1986.

again with signs of a trend towards greater use of multiple-rater systems (Fombrun and Laud 1983; Bernardin and Klatt 1985).

Who should appraise managers?

There are many potential appraisers of managers, both internal and external to the organization, and these are shown in box 3.7. We discuss each of these in turn.

Immediate manager

Traditional 'top-down' performance appraisal by the individual superior has often been described as an unsatisfactory, unrewarding and not particularly useful process for those involved. For example, Bush and Stinson describe it as 'an exercise in form filling and verbal confrontation' (1980: 17) and Teel as an 'unpleasant and ineffective necessity' (1978: 364).

Top-down performance appraisal has the potential to actually retard employee performance. A study by Kay et al. (1965) estimated that those on the receiving end of such appraisals, particularly where 'threats' are involved, may take as long as 12 weeks to regain their pre-appraisal levels of performance.

Box 3.7   Potential appraisers for managers

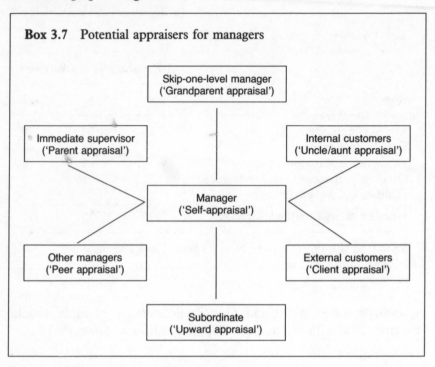

The problems associated with performance appraisal conducted by superiors are well documented. These include problems of reliability, validity, utility, practicality, and unintentional and intentional bias (Latham 1986). A key concern is that such appraisals are based only on the narrow and potentially unrepresentative sample of employee behaviours which superiors typically observe. However, the single-superior appraisal remains the most common approach. Why is this, in spite of calls for organizations to adopt a wider range of appraisers? At least three explanations have been offered.

Firstly, most appraising managers do not recognize the need for anyone other than themselves to be involved in the rating process. Secondly, and linked to this, appraising managers often wish to retain control of the appraisal process. Those managers responsible for appraisals seem to fear that if others were involved, this might lead to their losing influence over promotion decisions and other key issues. This is especially the case with the appraisal of managers, and we examine this issue in greater detail in the concluding section of this chapter. Thirdly, there are some advantages to parent-based appraisal systems: they are economical to operate, they underline that managers are responsible and accountable for the performance of their subordinates, and they are often found acceptable to those involved. But what are the alternatives?

Higher-level managers

The manager above the immediate superior can play an important role in appraisal. Occasionally, such managers act as primary appraisers, although this appears to be the exception, since the 'distance' from the appraisee limits the amount of first-hand knowledge about performance.

The more usual role for 'grandparent' managers is that of a reviewer of appraisals conducted by others, usually the immediate manager. This role is one of providing a safeguard against personal bias, inexperience, the adoption of incorrect procedures or the immediate manager 'forgetting' to conduct the appraisal at all. A further role is to hear individual appeals against adverse appraisals.

However, such grandparent review could introduce yet further bias into the process by pressurizing the immediate appraising manager into evaluating with two audiences in mind: the appraisee and the appraiser's manager. It seems that second-level reviewers often evaluate the appraising manager via the appraisals they conduct. For example, Patz (1975) found that if managers reported that all their employees were performing efficiently, this was interpreted by the grandparent reviewer as meaning either the manager was not aware of the employees' performance, could not differentiate between levels of employee ability, or that the manager was incapable of motivating improved performance. The danger is that the appraiser's manager becomes the primary audience, as a judge and appraiser of the manager conducting the appraisal, and that this compromises the entire process, so much so that the appraiser may not satisfy either audience (McGuire 1980).

Peer appraisal

There are three basic types of peer appraisal. Firstly, that of nomination, where each member of a managerial work group is asked to nominate one or more managers who they see as the highest on some particular aspect of performance. Nominations for the lowest performers are also sometimes requested and self-nominations are usually excluded. Secondly, there is the peer-ranking method, whereby the manager ranks the other managers from best to worst on one or more dimensions of performance. Thirdly, standard rating systems may be used, usually anonymously.

Research has generally been supportive of the use of peer appraisal. Peer assessments have been found to be sound in terms of the key properties of reliability and validity, to be a useful mechanism for differentiating between a manager's effort level and achievement outcomes, and to be effective in focusing on the most relevant abilities and competencies of those being rated (McEvoy and Buller 1987).

Peer review may be particularly appropriate for specialist professional staff, where only peers may possess the necessary technical expertise to make a credible assessment of performance. Further, professionals feel that they themselves are responsible for maintaining the performance standards of the profession and that performance appraisal by organizational managers may violate the principle of professional autonomy. The close teamwork involved in the work of professionals may also make peer review particularly appropriate.

In view of such favourable reports, it is surprising that peer appraisal is not very widespread. There are a number of possible reasons for this. Kane and Lawler (1978) suggest that peer reviews are perceived as amounting to little more than a 'popularity contest' and that this greatly undermines their credibility in the eyes of managers. Williams (1989) suggests that peer appraisal may create friction, damage interpersonal relationships, and erode trust amongst peers and is also subject to a friendship bias. For Williams, this limits the use of peer appraisal to a developmental role at most.

However, although there are no reported studies for managers, the experience of using peer appraisals for other groups has not always been negative. McEvoy and Buller's (1987) study of peer appraisal amongst process workers in a food plant found a majority of employees in favour of retaining the scheme in some form, although an earlier study of university professors had found the reverse (Cederbloum and Lounsbury 1980). One explanation for this difference in user acceptance may be that the system in the food processing plant was anonymous, unlike that in the university.

McEvoy and Buller suggest that in the food plant one of the reasons that employees supported the system was a feeling that peers would be likely to be 'easier' on them than would their immediate superior. Would this also be the case with managerial peer appraisal, particularly in the competitive world of middle managers? Research on actual cases of peer appraisal for managers is needed to throw more light on this question.

Self-appraisal

Regardless of whether or not the organization encourages it, self-appraisal will happen. People will always have a view on how well they are performing. Even those who have defended the use of more traditional systems of performance appraisal have stressed the need for greater involvement on the part of the appraisee (Patz 1975). Increasingly, it seems, organizations are heeding this advice and introducing an element of self-appraisal for managers, although in most cases this comprises only one part of the process.

Self-appraisal has several possible advantages. It may promote personal development, improve communication between managers and subordinates, clarify differences of opinion between managers, and overcome some of the problems of subjectivity. However, there is often a lack of agreement between self-ratings and those provided by other sources. It seems that individuals see their job performance differently than others, with a tendency towards leniency. Meyer et al. (1965) in a study of managers in the US General Electric Corporation found that on average each individual felt they were performing better than some 75 per cent of their peers and this tendency was more pronounced in senior managers. Later studies by Meyer (1980) found that 40 per cent of all employees consistently place themselves in the top 10 per cent of performers in anonymous self-appraisals, with up to 80 per cent of managers and professionals placing themselves in the top 10 per cent. Thus, self-appraisal for managers is particularly biased towards leniency.

Some, however, have argued that properly conducted self-appraisal may overcome this defect, particularly when it is used for developmental rather than evaluative purposes. A useful approach may be to require the manager to rate different aspects of performance against each other rather than against other managers, thus helping to eliminate the ranking bias and focus on areas for improvement.

Subordinate appraisal

Managers could be appraised by their subordinates. Sometimes referred to as 'upward appraisal' in the UK, or as 'reverse review' in the USA, this may avoid many of the problems associated with more traditional managerial appraisal systems. Upward appraisal appears to have originated in the USA, where it can be traced back to at least the 1960s. It has been less common in the UK, with the IPM surveys of the 1970s and 1980s failing to find a single organization that had adopted this practice. However, there have been some examples of its use in the UK in more recent years. W.H. Smith, BP Exploration, Rank Xerox, American Express UK, Avis and Federal Express have all announced the introduction of such schemes, with companies such as Gulf Oil and IBM having a long track record in this area.

In the UK, upward appraisal seems to be used mainly for feedback and developmental purposes, rather than for the more contentious areas of pay determination or promotion. However, there is some evidence of a broader use; for example, American Express is considering using upward appraisal for reward purposes.

Some organizations, for example ICI, use it as a basis for individualized management development plans. A number of business schools also use the upward appraisal of participants on their management development courses for similar purposes. The executive development programme at Henley uses feedback surveys from three of the participating managers' subordinates.

Upward appraisal has a number of strengths. Firstly, subordinates are usually in close contact with their managers and are thus in a position to observe directly a large volume of managerial behaviours. This allows them to observe and more accurately rate not only how the manager reacts in a crisis but also in more normal conditions. According to the head of management development at the US company, General Electric:

> They see him in good and bad times. They see how the individual hits for average, not just for home runs. (Baughman 1988: 19)

Secondly, subordinates are at the 'receiving end' of many managerial practices and this may give their observations greater validity for some aspects than those of top-down appraisers. The employee's perspective has tended to be a neglected area in the evaluation of HRM practices generally, but promises to provide valuable insights, not least in closing the 'perception gap' between a manager's view of his or her performance and that of the subordinates.

Thirdly, upward appraisal may be more valid than single-rater systems because it consists of more than one rating, because it is rarely conducted face to face, and because the anonymity of such an approach reduces the tendency toward leniency. Further, subordinate appraisal may be particularly effective in stimulating managers to take action in light of their appraisals, since feedback may be less easily ignored than with traditional downward appraisal, which may be rationalized away as the view of only one person who is not in particularly close contact with the manager (Tsui and Ohlott 1988).

There are, however, a number of reservations about the use of upward appraisal. It cannot be used to evaluate the full range of managerial performance, since many aspects such as decision making and goal setting are often not visible from the subordinate's perspective. Upward appraisal may therefore be more appropriate in evaluating the people-management aspects of managerial performance. Largely because of this, upward appraisal appears to be less accurate than other methods in predicting promotion potential to senior management positions (McEvoy and Beatty 1989).

The use of upward appraisal for evaluation as well as developmental purposes greatly reduces the acceptability of the process to the appraised managers. The introduction of upward appraisal of managers in the UK has not been without its difficulties and has necessitated the retraining of some 300 managers at W. H. Smith and the introduction of a counselling service at BP Exploration (see box 3.8).

Box 3.8   Upward appraisal at BP Exploration

BP Exploration decided to implement upward appraisal in conjunction with a number of other measures on performance management following a Management Forum in Arizona in 1990.

The underlying logic for its introduction stemmed from the company's view that responsibility for effective employee performance rests largely with line managers, irrespective of how sophisticated its HRM polices are. Following briefings and acceptance by managers and supervisors, the company launched the programme in late 1990, with some 1400 managers being appraised by 9000 employees, a participation rate of over 90 per cent.

Employees are asked to fill in detailed questionnaires requiring them to rate, on a scale of 1 to 5, the importance of some 23 'management practices' and then on the same scale to rate how well their managers have applied these. Managers are rated on such areas as ability to initiate change, capacity for taking tough decisions, how well they represent the views, opinions and feelings of staff up the line, their willingness to share power, and the maintenance of high standards for the unit's work, as well as their ability to promote BP Exploration's 'essential behaviours'. The latter include such qualities as tolerance, understanding others, team building and innovative thinking.

Individual responses are kept confidential and results are aggregated by external consultants, Forum Europe, who then go through the findings with each manager. Following this, meetings are set up between managers and employees to examine how they can best work with each other. This results in an input into the individual manager's 'Personal Action Plan' which might, for example, include a pledge by the manager to meet more regularly with staff. The action plan is then discussed with the manager's immediate manager and can be incorporated into the individual's objectives for the coming year.

One effect of upward appraisal at BP Exploration has been to close the 'perception gap' between a manager's view of his or her own performance and the views of their subordinates. This has caused some difficulties for the company's managers. On finding out what their employees really think of them some managers have experienced what BP Exploration have termed the SARAH process: Shock, Anger, Rejection, Acceptance and Help. These managers are then encouraged to seek counselling support from the company's consultants. Upward appraisal is not yet linked into the reward system for managers and supervisors, but the company sees this as a possibility for the future.

The programme is evaluated against its twin objectives, of ensuring that managers are 'walking as they talk' and of ensuring that those managers 'clearly not cut out to manage people are moved back into individual contribution roles' (Thomas et al. 1992: 32).

Sources: Creelman 1991; *Financial Times*, 4 June 1991: 7; Thomas et al. 1992.

Customers

Organizations are becoming more service- and customer-orientated. Accompanying this has been an increase in the attention paid to quality, most recently through TQM initiatives. Under TQM, the customer, whether internal or external to the organization, is supreme, and it thus seems a logical step to include customer evaluations of performance in the appraisal of managers. Performance appraisal can then play a key role in communicating to managers whether quality standards are being met. In some circumstances, customers may also provide an appropriate source of appraisal for an organization's professional employees, particularly for those whose jobs involve direct contact with clients, and where the client's acceptance of a professional's performance is critical (Von Ginlow 1990).

In the UK, there are few cases of a systematic use of external customers in the evaluation of managerial performance, except as a source of critical incidents used by the appraiser, and this is usually in the form of complaints. However, there is a growing use of 'mystery shoppers', whereby an individual, either a company employee or someone contracted in, poses as a customer or client and monitors and reports on the service encounter to senior managers. 'Mystery shoppers' are used in financial services and retailing, by Vauxhall to evaluate its dealer network, and also by BP Oil UK (Ring 1992). The Body Shop even use the shoppers' reports as a part of the criteria in determining performance-related pay. Whilst such appraisals are the exception rather than the rule at the moment, the spread of initiatives such as TQM and competitive benchmarking may lead to their more widespread use in the future.

In the USA, there is increasing evidence of the use of customer feedback in service industries to assess employees, including middle-level managers. Here, the control of middle managers via traditional bureaucratic systems is to some extent being replaced by one of managing managers by customers, since customers provide senior managers with a source of organizational power over the middle manager via a 'constant yet elusive presence' (Fuller and Smith 1991: 11).

Fuller and Smith's (1991) survey of service industries in the USA found extensive use of the 'mystery shopper' technique. Two of the companies even used shoppers that were 'wired', so that all interactions with the manager and employees could be picked up on microphone and recorded. The data derived from shoppers and the various surveys was routed into the personal files of managers to form the basis for performance evaluations. In some organizations this was collated and analysed by senior managers, and, as well as being used in formal performance appraisals, a league table of performance was posted. In one hotel group, senior corporate managers would write to middle managers receiving poor customer surveys with an analysis and give the manager 30 days to report to head office on how they had rectified the problem. In the absence of a satisfactory response, disciplinary action would ensue. Perhaps not surprisingly, such techniques were unpopular with managers and staff alike.

There are other problems with such systems. The data captured by customer feedback on middle management performance may be severely distorted, since many of the customer surveys have low response rates and are based on highly subjective data. In some cases, crude and perhaps dubious measures have been constructed to interpret the data. For example, a restaurant chain calculated the ratio of positive to negative remarks made by customers on comment cards. Some managers have reacted by collecting their own customer data, in order to check and perhaps challenge the analysis of senior managers.

Whilst appraisal by external customers is still rare in the UK, there are more examples of organizations using internal customers to evaluate managerial performance and commitment to specific programmes. A number of organizations, including ICI, make use of a manager's 'Uncle or Aunt', the manager's internal managerial customer, in performance reviews. Thus, rather than the personnel director alone rating the personnel manager's performance, the line managers receiving the services of the personnel manager would also have an input into the appraisal process.

Finally, it is worth noting that there is a possibility of conflict between traditional top-down appraisals and customer satisfaction and quality indicators. For example, a construction manager we interviewed was so enthused by his organization's introduction of TQM that he surveyed all his internal customers on his own initiative. He used an instrument devised and administered by himself and received an overall excellent rating. This caused him considerable concern when his immediate manager rated his performance as average on the organization's rating system.

Multiple appraisers

The above discussion suggests that there are potential benefits to both the organization and the manager in moving away from the traditional single-rater, top-down approach to appraisal. Multiple-rater systems may be recommended on the grounds that they give a more complete picture of a manager's performance and impact on others. In spite of this, such systems are not in widespread use. This is an area worthy of further development.

Managerial appraisal in practice: The hidden agenda?

In this section, we examine the micro-politics of managerial performance appraisal. In particular, we consider the evidence for a 'hidden agenda': that the process of appraisal acts as a bureaucratic defence mechanism to protect the prerogatives of senior line managers.

Although managerial appraisal systems are widespread, they are still often lacking in sophistication, especially in small and medium-sized companies. Many have pointed to the deficiencies of traditional performance appraisal systems. For example, Barlow describes appraisal as the 'routinized recording of trivialities' (1989: 503). Finn and Fontaine concluded on the basis of interviews with over a hundred managers that:

> With few exceptions interviewees displayed pronounced negative attitudes toward the performance appraisal process. It was considered to be a waste of time and seldom useful. (1983: 336)

For Barlow (1989), however, this is not merely the result of organizational inertia, incompetence, lack of training, or theoretical or technical deficiencies. Rather, it is a function of the hidden yet key role that managerial appraisal plays in the organizational politics of management. The limited benefit from performance appraisal, a process which promises so much in theory yet delivers so little in practice, obscures its latent organizational function: that of providing a bureaucratic defence of senior line managers' prerogatives over key decisions on management rewards. This is seen as a critical area, since if you want to win the hearts and minds of an organization's managers you must 'grab them by the careers' (with apologies to Gerald Ford).

Evidence for the political nature of managerial performance appraisal derives from a number of sources. For example, Longenecker et al. (1987) found managers adjusting their performance evaluations to achieve a wide variety of personal objectives. These included giving higher ratings to help a less able manager to be promoted 'up and out' of the department, lower ratings to teach a rebellious subordinate a lesson about 'who the boss is', and the sending of 'indirect messages' to certain managers that they should consider leaving.

In our own study of a medium-sized financial services organization, we found a system of managerial promotion that was determined not by the formal mechanisms of the performance appraisal system, which was extensive and demanded a great deal of management time and effort, but by an informal system dominated by senior line managers (Snape et al. 1993). In this case, there was much criticism of the promotion process by middle managers, with a majority of them also expressing dissatisfaction with the conduct of their own performance appraisal. The most common complaint from managers was that the formal performance appraisal process was merely a 'paper exercise', 'a rubber stamp job' that was only given 'lip service' by those involved. In particular, it was the fact that the appraisal data did not appear to be used which most frustrated managers and undermined the value of the process in the eyes of many. This view is illustrated by the comments of a number of managers:

> The way the interview goes, I get the idea that it's a once a year paper exercise and then the forms are signed off and stashed away. They might be read, but there is no real notice taken of them.

> The ideas you put down on the form are there for ever rather than actually being taken on in any real way.

> I cannot imagine anyone at head office reads them at all.

> . . . appraisal forms are just stored away by personnel. I do not know if anybody else reads them.

Yet in spite of such views, we found senior line managers to be generally supportive of the appraisal process, and few expressed any desire to end or limit its use. Similarly, Patz's (1975) study of performance appraisal found that managers were unwilling to discard formal systems despite considerable difficulty in carrying them out.

Given the strategic importance attached to management careers, it appears that, in some organizations at least, decisions on this issue are much too significant to be left to the vagaries of performance appraisal. Key decisions over managerial careers are taken outside the performance appraisal process by senior line managers in a form of organizational patronage (Barlow 1989). In practice, the essential role of performance appraisal is to obscure this process and to provide a rational and objective veneer to career decisions. It thus supplies an organizational defence mechanism against internal challenge by the unfavoured, by-passed and aggrieved manager.

Performance appraisal also has the potential to provide evidence of a rational process if legally challenged by such managers. So far, legal challenges to performance appraisal have been largely confined to North America (Latham 1986). Townley (1990), however, has argued that legal challenge is increasingly likely to be an issue in the UK. A recent industrial tribunal case won by a demoted British Gas manager involved an examination of performance appraisal data, and may herald a move towards legalism in the UK (*Financial Times*, 10 March 1992: 9).

Is this view of managerial performance appraisal as nothing more than an organizational defence mechanism applicable to most organizations? There is a danger of generalizing from a limited number of cases, but increasingly research evidence seems to support this position. If this is the case, is it a problem, and if so what solutions can be applied? These questions remain unresearched but, as we showed earlier, the use of multiple-raters offers some potential to move beyond the trivial in managerial appraisal, and it may be that such an approach could also depoliticize the appraisal process by widening the responsibility for appraisal beyond senior managers.

Some, however, would argue that rather than attempt the difficult task of removing politics from the appraisal process, organizations should manage the role that it plays. The view here is that the search for accuracy is a futile and pointless task as managers will always use an appraisal system for their own ends. Organizations should recognize this and try to ensure that such manipulations of the appraisal process add to rather than detract from organizational effectiveness (Longenecker et al. 1987). However, managing the politics of managerial appraisal is far easier to suggest than to achieve, given its largely hidden nature. Only more research on performance appraisal in practice, rather than the laboratory, will allow us to determine whether the political processes involved in appraising managers is indeed manageable.

Summary and conclusions

In this chapter, we have argued that managerial performance appraisal is important but is often flawed in practice. Before introducing or when reviewing managerial appraisal systems, organizations need to ask some very basic though often troublesome questions. We conclude the chapter by reviewing these.

- *Should we bother with appraisal?* In most cases the answer to this question will be 'yes'. However, it is important that expectations are realistic. There is a danger of seeing appraisal as the answer to all an organization's management problems. A soundly based system that receives commitment from senior managers can make a worthwhile contribution to the management of managers, but appraisal is expensive and time consuming to introduce and maintain. Computerization may help to ease the administrative burden.

- *What should we use it for?* Those responsible for the design of systems will need to carefully consider the aims of performance appraisal in their organization. Increasingly, organizations try to link performance appraisal with decisions on remuneration, promotion, succession planning and management development. Particularly prominent is the move to performance-related pay as organizations seek to encourage more entre-preneurial behaviour amongst managers (see chapter 6). The danger is that multiple objectives can conflict, and there may be a need to make some choices here.

- *Who should appraise managers?* We recommend that organizations consider multiple-rater systems for managers. In addition to the immediate superior, at the very least there should be a role for self-appraisal. Serious consideration should also be given to peer appraisal, particularly for professional employees, and upward appraisal for managers with employees reporting directly to them.

- *How should we appraise our managers?* There are several possible approaches. Some, such as trait ratings and ranking schemes, usually have little to recommend them, particularly for managers. Along with multiple appraisers, we would endorse a multiple-method approach to managerial appraisal, which could incorporate some form of self-reporting, the setting of performance objectives, and ratings anchored to observable managerial behaviour. The use of systematic organization-based competency models has considerable potential.

- *How do we implement and maintain appraisal?* Appraisal requires careful introduction and preparation. This requires a strong communications effort on the nature of the scheme, and a supportive skills-based training programme for appraisers and appraisees. Maintenance of appraisal systems is also important, and complex systems requiring managers to complete large volumes of paperwork soon fall into disrepute. Care must be taken that simple, user-friendly and useful systems remain so. However, the appraisal process should not be reduced to the mere ticking of meaningless boxes. This is a question of balance.

Appraisal systems of the future, like the organizations in which they will be used, need to be flexible enough to accommodate major changes in the environment and to support rather than hinder organizational goals. Likely future developments include an increasing use of customer-generated data in the appraisal of managers, the internationalization of appraisal systems to accommodate a global managerial workforce, and a general increase in the importance of appraisal in securing the motivation and commitment of managers in flatter organizational structures as traditional promotion pathways contract.

Further reading

A discussion of the principles of performance appraisal can be found in Peter Herriot (ed.), *Assessment and Selection in Organisations*, Chichester: Wiley, 1989. A study of the practice of performance appraisal is Phil Long, *Performance Appraisal Revisited*, London: Institute of Personnel Management, 1986.

4
Management Training and Development

In the late 1980s, two major reports suggested that UK managers enjoyed less systematic education and training than those in many other countries (Constable and McCormick 1987; Handy 1987). Constable and McCormick estimated that UK managers received only one day's training per year on average, with most managers receiving no training at all in any given year. Handy compared this to the USA, where 42 per cent of the top 500 companies gave their managers more than five days off-the-job training per year. Handy also suggested that British managers were under-educated compared to managers in other countries, with fewer having university degrees.

The Handy and the Constable and McCormick reports recommended that provision of management education be expanded, that ease of access should be improved, and that there should be closer liaison between employers and educational institutions. They exhorted employers to recruit with greater care and to use appraisal systems to encourage an emphasis on continuing training and development. Individual managers were urged to take a keener interest in their own training and development. The Handy report suggested that large employers should establish a declared target of five days off-the-job training per year, and the hope was that high-profile employers would emerge as leaders in improving the quality of managerial training and development and thereby set an example to others.

In response to this challenge, the National Forum for Management Education and Development, the Confederation of British Industry and then British Institute of Management launched the Management Charter Initiative (MCI), designed to 'increase the quality and professionalism of managers at all levels throughout the economy' (see below).

This concern with management training and development has not been restricted to the UK. Other countries have had similar debates, not least because there is a growing recognition of the importance of human resources as a contributor to competitiveness. Increased international competition has forced organizations to reconsider their approaches to their human resources and to achieve more from them in an economically efficient way, whilst technological change has brought pressing training needs.

In this chapter, we examine the context of management development, its objectives, and some of the main techniques used. We then examine the contribution of employers and of business schools, looking in particular at the changing role of the MBA qualification. The chapter concludes with a review of some recent developments, concentrating on the management competency debate and initiatives to develop the 'international manager'.

Training and development in the UK: A quiet revolution?

Whilst the Handy and the Constable and McCormick reports were useful in focusing attention on training and development, it is important not to sound too despairing of the UK's performance in this area. International comparisons in management training and education are to some extent simply a reflection of the traditional British approach, whereby managers tend to be qualified in a specific function such as accountancy, engineering or computing, rather than being trained in management as such.

Furthermore, there is evidence that the educational level of British managers has improved in recent years (Mansfield and Poole 1991: 13), and the expansion of business and management education suggests that British management is improving its expertise. More employers are beginning to see training and development as having a key role to play in meeting new needs and adapting to a changing environment (see, for example, box 4.1). Many are experimenting with new techniques in management development, on-the-job training, mentoring, coaching, personal development plans, and development workbooks (Storey et al. 1991). It also appears that managers themselves are increasingly recognizing the need for training and development (Mansfield and Poole 1991; Warr 1993).

However, while there are some positive signs, a number of concerns remain (Storey et al. 1991). Management development is often

Box 4.1   Management development in Britain's National Health Service

The NHS has been subject to a number of major changes in recent years, including large scale reorganization in 1974 and 1982, and the introduction of general management in 1985. However, the most fundamental change was the introduction of competition via the mechanism of internal markets. Self-governing Hospital Trusts, for example, now enjoy much greater freedom to manage their resources, and to set their own staff budgets and determine staff contracts. This has contributed to a marked increase in the number of managers.

This new commercial environment has made new demands on management. Training and development has hitherto been somewhat neglected in the NHS (it was described as having been a 'Cinderella' function by one NHS personnel manager we interviewed), but has now become a critical business concern. One indication of this is the 'Strategic Human Resource Development Initiative' launched by the NHS Training Authority in 1990.

Health authorities and trusts set up management development departments and organizational development functions. Management development and training consultants are also more widely used. Many new initiatives have emerged.

For example, development-focused assessment centres are now used extensively, and each region has its own assessment criteria and competency profiles. South-east Thames, for example, put its top 1000 managers through an assessment and development process to identify and remedy critical skill gaps. Action learning sets, based on the work of Revans, have been developed by Yorkshire Health Authority, who have also set up a lunchtime 'management club', meeting monthly with invited speakers from inside and outside the organization. In 1993, the Northern Regional Health Authority launched a specific health sector MBA programme for its managers, in collaboration with Durham University.

A particular challenge is that of training medical professionals who have now become much more involved in management. Doctors and nurses, for example, are traditionally provided with little or no management training as part of their initial professional education. Some – for example, Milton Keynes Hospital – have addressed this by providing management training to doctors, nurses and administrators on the same courses. The Milton Keynes Hospital has taken the integration of management training one step further. An intensive three week course has been developed, in conjunction with a local college, and involving management simulations and outdoor development. This was designed primarily for the hospital's own staff, but has also been opened up to employees of the local authority and voluntary agencies.

Sources: Arkin 1991a; Tietjen 1991; and interviews with NHS managers.

not effectively linked with human resource planning systems, nor accepted as a legitimate line management activity, usually being seen as the responsibility of training and development specialists. Employers' commitment to continuous development is still limited, and management development is often imbued with a 'sink or swim' philosophy: managers either have what it takes, and thus need little development, or they have not, in which case management development activities would be wasted.

Storey et al. (1991) suggest that management development in the UK still relies too much on sending managers on courses, rather than encouraging self-development. There is a marked tendency for British management development to fall victim to 'programmitis', with a constant series of newly launched programmes and initiatives with little consistency. Thus, managers often get little more than a chance to attend the latest company campaign, be it TQM, performance management, or whatever is the current flavour of the month.

Too often, this is done with little attention to the training and development needs of the individual. Management training thus reduces to the 'sheep dip' approach; all managers go through it whether they need it or not. As a line manager we interviewed put it:

They do not look at an individual and say 'We will do this for you'. They decide that time management is a good thing and everyone does it.

Management training and development: What are we trying to achieve?

There are several reasons why organizations should invest in management training and development. Firstly, it reduces the need to recruit skilled managers from outside the organization and may induce loyalty to the organization and reduce turnover. Secondly, an organization with a good reputation for training and development is often able to attract the best recruits. Thirdly, in today's uncertain corporate environment, organizations increasingly rely on having flexible staff who are able to respond to change, so that managers may need training throughout their careers.

Training programmes may be *anticipatory*: intended to meet long-term organizational objectives; *reactive*: intended to pre-empt difficulties; and *motivational*: intended to satisfy individual career aspirations and to promote job satisfaction more generally (BCA 1990).

The most effective training and development programmes exhibit certain characteristics: they are endorsed and promoted by senior management; they are integrated with and informed by the organization's strategic plan; the training chosen takes into account the development needs of the individual; the training method is appropriate for the skill or attribute being developed; training is regarded as continuous; and it is evaluated and reviewed regularly (Sadler 1989).

It is important to analyse training needs prior to conducting the training. Managerial training needs can be analysed at the level of the organization, the job and the individual. In an organizational-needs analysis, the organization's demand for human resources and skills is derived from an examination of corporate objectives, the efficiency of the organization, and the corporate culture, turnover and productivity.

A job-needs analysis entails setting performance standards, describing tasks to be completed and optimal procedures for performing these, and specifying the requisite knowledge and skills for task performance. An individual-needs analysis seeks to identify particular managers' training needs via performance appraisals, assessment centres and other methods of measuring job performance (see chapters 3 and 5). Ideally, there is an overlap between the individual's and the organization's aspirations, and an individual's training-needs analysis has to be reconciled with the job-needs and the organizational-needs analyses.

In practice, the analysis of training needs is often far from systematic (Holden 1991; O'Driscoll and Taylor 1992). Ad hocery and informality appear to dominate over systematic analysis, with casual observation, production problems, customer complaints and self requests being the main methods by which managers' training needs are diagnosed. For example, Saari et al.'s (1988) survey of management training in the USA found that only a quarter of organizations had formal procedures for determining the training needs of their managers. One consequence is that management training is often poorly targeted and fails to change individual behaviour or contribute to improved organizational performance (Kubr and Prokopenko 1989).

A proactive management development programme, which is informed by the strategic plan and integrated with the other elements of the HRM cycle, may provide a powerful tool for the organization to achieve its strategic longer-term goals (Osbaldeston and Barham 1992). Central to this requirement is a human resources development (HRD) function which is well informed about, and preferably has influence upon, strategic planning. Forward planning and knowledge of the long-term strategy of the organization allows the HRD function to ensure that sufficient people are trained ready for new initiatives. Prior knowledge also allows the HRD function to avoid spending time and money training people for roles which the organization plans to discontinue. Again, however, the practice often falls short of the ideal, with few organizations linking their management training needs analysis with their strategic planning (O'Driscoll and Taylor 1992).

Management training and development techniques

The appropriate training and development method will depend to a great extent on the particular development need. For example, lectures may be suitable where the aim is to provide a large amount of basic knowledge or information to a number of trainees in a cost-effective manner. Role-play, case studies and simulations, however, are more useful in developing applied skills and in influencing attitudes (Anderson 1992).

Two main approaches to training and development can be distinguished. Firstly, an *andragogical* approach is essentially self-directed, whereby learning is trainee driven, collaborative, participative, and where the trainer's role is largely supportive rather than judgemental. Secondly, *pedagogical* approaches are largely trainer-driven and authority orientated.

Delahaye (1992) uses the andragogy/pedagogy distinction to devise a grid of training techniques or strategies to match the management competency being developed. The techniques of self-managed

learning – for example, contract learning, action learning and problem solving – exhibit low pedagogy and high andragogy and are
useful techniques for developing mental agility, creativity and self-
knowledge, the key qualities which underpin the acquiring of all
other skills. Here, individuals take personal responsibility for their
learning by selecting goals, appropriate methods and evaluating their
learning. This approach to management development encourages
experimentation, gives individuals autonomy, questions the status
quo and is tolerant of mistakes. The lecture, by contrast, shows high
pedagogy and low andragogy, and although it may be useful for
imparting basic knowledge and information, is limited in terms of its
ability to develop skills.

Where managers are constantly faced with new challenges, they
need to learn how to learn. Thus, whatever teaching/learning method
is used, the manager should leave the programme equipped to put
into effect what has been learned and to draw further applications
from it in new and challenging situations. This need for the learning
to be brought back into the organization and applied in practical
conditions has informed the current debate about appropriate techniques of management training and about the development of the
learning company (Pedler et al. 1991).

In the rest of this section, we discuss a selection of management
training and development techniques. Our aim is to discuss examples
of each broad approach, and to illustrate some of the more interesting
innovations.

Computer-assisted learning

Computer-assisted learning (CAL) and computer-based education
can be considered as a blending of pedagogy and andragogy, since
the learning is programmed but the trainees, through the flexibility
and sophistication of the program, can proceed at their own pace and
location. It can be conducted at work, at home, in remote locations
or even while travelling.

CAL may be particularly appropriate for learning impersonal
techniques (such as discounted cash flow), rather than for people-
management skills (such as conducting selection or performance
appraisal interviews). However, programs for the latter have also
been developed. For example, Maxim have produced packages in
such areas as interviewing skills, the management of change, leadership skills, negotiating skills, and performance troubleshooting.

Some CAL packages have been criticized for being little more than electronic books. At their worst, such programs offer a pre-test and post-test, but in between the manager does little more than press the 'page down' key. At their best, CAL programs go well beyond this, and can involve the trainee in a high level of interaction.

Role-playing

This technique allows a high degree of involvement by the learner and possibly by the trainer. The aim is to create a realistic situation in which the manager assumes a specific role. The participants receive role briefs, outlining the roles to be played, the personal backgrounds of the characters and the situational background. However, participants are usually given a degree of freedom to develop the characters and the events as they wish.

The trainee experiences the problems and issues in a quasi-realistic manner and the trainer can further enrich the learning by encouraging group discussion. The method can be used in a number of ways, for example in behaviour modelling where managers are shown the desired behaviour, perhaps on video, and then perform a role-play to practise the skills for themselves.

Role-playing can be especially appropriate in training managers in people-handling skills, such as selection and appraisal interviewing, and negotiating (see, for example, Perry 1992). A reversal of day-to-day job roles within a role play may also help managers to recognize and counter personal bias, and to reflect on their day-to-day job performance. *Now go back to written notes*

One particular type of role play used in management development is where junior managers sit on a 'shadow' or 'junior' board of directors which makes recommendations on organization-wide issues. The participants gain experience in policy-making earlier than would otherwise be possible. However, junior boards have not been widely adopted. One of the main drawbacks is that they have no responsibility or accountability and this results in the discussions lacking identifiable outputs and actions, and leads to feelings of 'psychological and managerial impotence' amongst participants (Mumford 1989: 124).

Case studies

The case-study method is based on the belief that people learn well by focusing on a specific problem or issue. Participants may be divided into small groups to consider the problem and associated questions, with reports back to a plenary session, so that the various insights are shared. Participants are encouraged to draw on their own experience. They are thus involved in their own tuition and are better able to develop their analytical, critical and discursive competencies. Role-playing parts of the case study often further enhances understanding, while developing negotiating, interviewing, public speaking and teamworking skills. A major use is to demonstrate the possibility of multiple courses of action in a particular situation.

The case-study method relies on skilful guidance of the group by the trainer, who acts as facilitator and catalyst. When using both role-playing and case studies, it is essential for the trainer to clarify the learning objectives and key points, before and after the exercise. Group discussions beforehand and structured feedback are thus critical to the successful use of both of these methods.

Management games and simulations

These simulate aspects of a management situation and often involve participants working in a team in competition with others to achieve a stated goal, such as maximizing sales, profits etc. Games may involve the transfer of information, and the development of teamworking. Where role-playing is involved, they can also increase self- and social awareness.

Some of the more sophisticated applications of simulations combine their use with a manager's own Personal Action Plan to reinforce learning and improve performance, in line with corporate priorities. ICI has used simulation to develop a more market-focused culture amongst managers. In the USA, General Electric has used simulation to introduce the managers of a recently acquired Hungarian company to the skills needed in managing in a market economy (Thorne 1992).

Simulations have the advantage of being exciting, realistic, useful for integrating learning across a number of management functions, and of encouraging managers to apply skills and techniques. However, they are often expensive to run, require high participant commitment, and are unpredictable, as every run of a simulation may be different. They are also criticized for their inability to replicate real-life conditions. Another problem is their tendency to over-emphasize competitive behaviour. Management functions which in real life depend heavily on cooperative behaviour and teamwork often become fiercely competitive in management games (Long and Tonks 1991).

Action learning

The assumption underlying action learning is that learning occurs from a combination of programmed knowledge (P) and questioning insight (Q) (Revans 1987). A good action-learning programme emphasizes the Q element more than the P element, leading to independent thought and individual development. A typical programme involves a short period of education in basic subjects such as finance, organizational management and communications, after which participants are assigned a real-life problem to solve. Projects are chosen which offer a challenge, but which are soluble within a reasonable time frame.

The participants meet regularly in small groups to discuss their progress and share knowledge and ideas, and derive mutual support. The programme takes place over a specified time period, and the learner's solution is put into effect. Participants then review the effectiveness of the action taken and derive lessons from others' projects as well as from their own.

Outdoor training

Much modern management activity involves teamwork, and yet managers' education has often emphasized individualistic and competitive behaviour rather than group-orientated and cooperative behaviour. Outdoor training, first introduced in the Second World War as a means of developing skills and the will to survive amongst seafarers, nowadays represents an attempt to develop team building and leadership skills. Hogg (1988a) lists some 18 applications of outdoor training in management development, including improving communications, encouraging creativity, helping participants cope with stress, and improving interpersonal, planning, decision-making, and time-management skills. It may also help revitalize a flagging management team.

One estimate suggests that in the UK the supply of outdoor training courses doubled every five years in the 1980s (Lowe 1991). A recent survey suggested that outdoor training was being used by 50 per cent of large UK employers (Industrial Relations Services 1992). British Rail, Rolls Royce, British Airways, Shell

Box 4.2   Outdoor management development at Exxon Chemical

In the UK, Exxon Chemical, a division of the American company Exxon, has used outdoor development for many years. Recently, it has extended its use of the outdoors from graduate recruits and junior staff to mainstream management development. In part, this was triggered by the launch in the USA of a major corporate values programme, 'Quest', which made a successful use of outdoor development. Several programmes have since been set up in the UK to cascade the new corporate values throughout the company. One of these, 'Choices', is aimed at European middle managers.

Choices is run in conjunction with a specialist outdoor consultancy firm. The outdoor element is part of a wider programme incorporating both pre- and post-course work. The objectives for managers participating in Choices are:

• to develop an understanding of the company's core values;
• to increase awareness of teamworking and the value of diversity and leadership;
• to develop personal action plans to put the core values into practice at work;
• to develop teamworking and networking on company projects.

Prior to the course, participants are asked to consider their feelings about the company's core values, complete a questionnaire on this, and discuss them with their managers and colleagues.

During the programme, outdoor exercises and projects are used to mirror management situations and challenges. Each exercise focuses on a different company core value such as leadership, diversity, teamwork and partnership. The exercises progress from the straightforward to the complex, requiring high levels of cooperation, organization and innovation. Each exercise is followed by a debrief and review period, in which performance is evaluated, strengths and weaknesses are examined and future strategies planned. During the course, participants develop their own personal action plan linked to the company values and develop a team or network project to help the organization achieve its mission.

Participation in Choices is voluntary. In part, this is to deal with managers' concerns about being fit enough to face the physical challenge.

Source: Industrial Relations Services 1991c.

and Marks and Spencer in the UK; Telecom, BHP and Alcoa in Australia; and Exxon (see box 4.2) and Apple Computers in the USA, are amongst those using the outdoors for management development.

Typically, participants work in teams, on tasks involving obstacles of distance, terrain and weather. Proponents of the method argue that it promotes team spirit, highlights the need for effective organizing, planning and communication, and develops self-confidence. However, the context is so radically different from the workplace that there are doubts about such learning being transferred to the organization. According to one commentator:

> The glossy brochures from the increasing number of consultancies and others in the field emphasize broad horizons: trampling across windswept moors, inching up a vertical rockface in the middle of nowhere, getting from one side of the chasm to the other, rowing a whaleboat into the unknown. All are no doubt worthy pursuits. But what evidence do we have that such activities are reliable in meeting their objectives? The answer, unfortunately, must be 'not a lot'. (James 1989: 18)

Outdoor training is usually expensive, requiring a high tutor–participant ratio, and direct costs range from £300 to over £2000 per manager per course (Hogg 1988a). Some organizations also have reservations about suddenly transferring a middle-aged manager from a sedentary job to a tough outdoor training course, where there are dangers to be confronted, not least those of heart failure!

Job rotation/secondment

On-the-job training has long been the main approach to management training in Britain and elsewhere, with a traditional emphasis on 'sitting by Nellie' and learning by experience (see box 4.3). Such traditional approaches may be criticized for being unsystematic, for passing on bad practice, and as being costly in terms of possible errors made whilst learning. However, they have the advantage of realism, and it is likely that any new manager will undergo an element of learning on the job, no matter how thorough the pre-job training. Furthermore, a planned sequence of job moves is a highly effective form of long-term development.

Recruits into management training programmes have often passed through a brief phase of job rotation before moving into a specific function such as HRM, marketing or production. This is now being

---

Box 4.3   Managerial learning in the school of hard knocks

Many have traditionally argued that to become a good manager requires learning the hard way – by experience – rather than through
formal education and training. We all at some time suffer distressing
events which can also provide valuable learning experiences – what
might be called the 'school of hard knocks' approach to management
development.

Snell identifies a pattern of outcomes from hard knocks. These
include simply coming to terms with the distressful event, developing
an expedient coping strategy, or actually learning from it.

Typical 'hard knocks' include managers hitting impasses, suffering
defeats and injustices, coming under personal attack, making the 'big
mistake', and being overstretched. Hard knocks can be turned to the
manager's advantage by resisting the reprisal urge, 'cooling off' and
learning from the distress. Learning can be achieved by, for example,
seeking counselling, conducting post-mortems, and obtaining fair
criticism.

Source: Snell 1989.

---

extended in many organizations as the value of flexibility is realized.
This is a particularly strong feature of Japanese-style on-the-job
management development. Such an approach may involve transfer,
job rotation, or secondment inside or outside the organization.

Increasingly, the public sector is using secondment to private-
sector organizations to develop more entrepreneurial managers. Companies such as ICI, Shell, the major clearing banks and other 'blue
chip' organizations have long used secondment schemes. In some
cases these are 'terminal secondments', as part of a transition towards
outplacement or retirement. The IPM has recently produced a code
of practice on the use of secondments to achieve maximum benefit
to seconder, secondee and host organization. Where secondments
are used as part of management development, the development
opportunities may be wasted if care is not taken in managing the re-
entry of the trainee.

Overseas assignments are an especially challenging type of transfer,
offering rich experience for those managers seeking career advancement. However, such postings are costly, and may therefore be
dictated by local operational needs rather than by the development
needs of an individual.

Mentoring

Mentoring normally involves a senior manager acting as mentor to a more junior manager. There are various roles that a mentor can adopt. Hunt and Michael (1983) identify those of godfather, sponsor, guide, peer pal and role model. Akande (1992) on the other hand suggests that a mentor is a cross between teacher, uncle, wet nurse, cousin, guru and sugar daddy.

The junior manager may refer to the mentor on a wide range of work-related issues. The mentor is able to advise the trainee on appropriate responses to various managerial problems, and provides a role model for the less-experienced manager. Where mentoring takes place throughout the organization this may sustain the organization's culture (this might of course be seen as either a positive or a negative thing!).

Many of the more subtle interpersonal problems faced by the inexperienced manager may be readily solved after discussion with an experienced mentor, and the trainee may gain an insight into the thinking of higher-level management – all of which can lead to accelerated learning and greater awareness of the wider context within which the manager works. Also, the junior manager's career may gain from the support of a more powerful and politically wise mentor.

In some situations, a trainee or junior manager may understudy the person they are subsequently to replace, who thereby acts as a trainer for the specific job. The junior manager may take over elements of the senior's job. This technique is useful in succession planning, but its success is dependent on the quality of their relationship and on the senior's tutoring abilities.

A major disadvantage of mentoring is that it can be time consuming for senior managers. It is important that mentors are themselves given training, as the role is particularly demanding and complicated, requiring excellent interpersonal skills. There is also the issue of finding appropriate mentors for women managers, given their under-representation in senior management and possible differences in management style between women and men managers.

Management learning contracts

A management learning contract (MLC) is a written agreement made between a participating manager and the trainer, setting out what and how the manager wishes to learn. The contracting approach has its origins in the US educational system. It permits the trainee to have a hand in designing the programme and thus ensures relevance. It involves the trainee accepting the responsibility to learn, enhances the motivation to learn, and commits the trainee to action.

In the UK, the use of MLCs is most closely associated with the work of the Northern Regional Management Centre, where the approach has been successfully used for a wide range of purposes, including the retraining of unemployed managers, junior and middle management programmes, and MBA programmes (Boak 1991). A typical MLC specifies the following in writing:

- Goal – the overall direction or title of the contract or series of contracts.
- Learning objectives – to be achieved at the end of the contract period.
- Activities – what will be done to reach the objectives.
- Resources – required information or time needed to reach objectives.
- Assessment – what the participant will produce as evidence that the contract has been completed successfully.
- Time – a deadline for the assessment.

The agreement of the contract is a critical phase in the successful use of MLCs. Ideally, this should involve the manager, the manager's boss and the trainer. The contract needs to be precise, realistic and achievable, given the available time and resources. It is important to avoid an overemphasis on tasks to be completed rather than learning objectives to be achieved.

In-house training and development

Having considered the techniques of management training and development, we now address the issue of who actually provides it. We begin by looking at in-house provision, and in the following section we discuss the contribution of the business schools.

Many employers provide their own in-house management development, perhaps using external consultants such as chambers of commerce, employers' organizations, management consultants and educational institutions in conjunction with their own specialists. For example, in the UK, Unilever, the Civil Service, British Steel and GEC each have their own management colleges (see box 4.4), as do large US companies such as Aetna Insurance and A.D. Little.

The advantage of in-house provision is that it can be more easily tailored to meet the specific needs of the organization. The argument

---

Box 4.4 Training for the market

Increasingly, company-specific management training centres are turning to the open market as well as providing management training for their parent company. Dunchurch, the GEC management college, is one of the largest post-experience management centres in the UK and provides its facilities and expertise not only to all GEC companies but also to industry, commerce and the public sector.

Participants in Dunchurch programmes can build a bespoke MSc or MBA, or alternatively claim credit for units taken against other providers' qualifications, under the Credit Accumulation and Transfer Scheme (CATS). For example, the college has recently introduced a course to develop the commercial staff of its clients, covering such areas as prospecting and opportunity analysis, negotiating, contracting, financing and exporting. The programme has been accredited by Coventry University for the award of a postgraduate Diploma in Management.

---

against is that organization-specific courses may lack the broader perspective found on many external courses, such as those offered by the university business schools (see below). However, some argue that their organizations are so large and diverse that their managers can rely on the various strategic business units to provide new and stimulating approaches.

The MBA and the business schools

In 1986, Britain had 47 business schools, turning out some 2500 MBAs a year. By 1992, this had grown to 92 business schools, awarding around 5800 MBAs annually. This was more than the rest of Europe combined, although still proportionately fewer than the USA. However, the MBA is spreading from its Anglo-Saxon origins into continental Europe and into Asia. Although fewer European business schools award MBAs, there are some well-established ones, including INSEAD in France and IMEDE in Switzerland. Business schools have also grown rapidly in Eastern Europe. For example, Prague, Budapest, St Petersburg, Kracow and Moscow now all have one. British and American business schools have been at the centre of Eastern European developments.

The surveys find that most people take an MBA to try to improve their promotion prospects, or to change career direction. However, MBA graduates are not necessarily assured of immediate employment on graduating, particularly during a recession, in spite of business schools' attempts to market their graduates to prospective employers. This message appears to be reaching MBA students. The CNAA's 1991 survey of UK MBA students found that graduates felt that the main benefits of an MBA are its general education value and its contribution to personal development, rather than any direct contribution to work skills or career development.

Many criticisms have been levelled at management education, and at the business schools in particular. Common criticisms include rigidity of thinking, complacency, offering generalized platitudes and having a largely functionally based approach to management development, with insufficient recognition of the fact that today's managers must work across traditional functional boundaries (Ashton 1988; Warner 1990). Women are generally under-represented on MBAs, and business schools have been criticized for being slow to recognize their role in marketing management as a woman's career (Sinclair and Hintz 1991). The product of the business school, the MBA graduate, has also been criticized. For example, British employers are often reported as seeing MBA graduates as being too theoretical in their thinking and better at formulating strategies than making things happen.

Latterly, there has been more sensitivity to client needs in the design of MBA programmes. Since the mid-1980s, business schools have diversified in the type of MBA course offered, the location and manner of learning. The first change was to more part-time courses, which were welcomed by employers. However, many managers work until late in the evening, frequently travel away from home and have to relocate periodically, so it is difficult for some to attend regular classes over a period of years. Therefore, several MBAs are now taught by some form of distance-learning.

Many courses are now offering specializations; for example, in financial management, marketing, HRM or international management. Thus, the proliferation of MBA courses has been accompanied by attempts to design courses to fill particular market niches. MBA courses are also being taught to overseas management students by UK-based business schools in cooperation with local institutions; for example, Bath School of Management provides an MBA in conjunction with the Malaysian Institute of Management.

Along with increased variety of content and a more international focus, there has been a trend towards more participative and self-directed forms of learning, and away from the more traditional structured and directed lecture, seminar or guided reading approaches of the past. Some business schools have adopted a largely project-based approach, the projects being real issues to be resolved within an organization. Project-based action learning has become more widespread.

Some employers recognize the value of an MBA course in providing their managers with a broader appreciation of the business environment and management functions, and yet prefer not to send managers on a general course that may appear remote from the concerns of their own organization, with its distinctive culture, values and strategies. Thus, many have opted for an in-company programme, which provides an MBA level of knowledge and skills, whilst also being tailored to suit the needs of the particular organization. These and other advantages, such as improving morale and retention of key managers, have led to considerable growth in the 'bespoke' MBA sector. In 1989, some 15 such programmes enrolled 500 managers in the UK.

Typically, with the in-company MBA, the client organization is considered to be an equal partner with the business school, and is involved in course design, selection of participants, the provision of work-based projects, and formulation of assessment strategy. The mode of delivery is structured to meet the needs of the employer. For example, in-company MBAs can be provided in short intensive blocks, long weekends or more traditional modes such as evening classes supplemented with short residential courses.

A number of aspects appear critical to the success of in-company MBAs. Firstly, it is essential that the employer recognizes the philosophical difference between an MBA, with its emphasis on generalism, theory as well as practice, and critical awareness; and that of the typical in-house training course, which is more likely to be purely practice-based, often with a 'one best way' approach (Ashton 1989). Secondly, contractual arrangements should be clear. For example, it must be clear what happens to those participants who leave the sponsoring organization during the course, but who wish to complete their MBA. Thirdly, the company itself should have sufficient diversity to provide the breadth of learning experience that is a hallmark of the open programme MBA.

Some UK organizations have avoided some of the costs involved in an exclusive in-house MBA by cooperating with other organizations in a consortium MBA, in collaboration with a university business school. The members of the consortium all benefit from a cross-fertilization of ideas and experiences. Some of the consortia have very diverse participants: for example, the Warwick University consortium includes BP, Coopers and Lybrand, the Metropolitan Police, and the NatWest Bank. In the Warwick course, managers must carry out at least two of their four assignments in an organization other than their own (Hogg 1988b). Other consortia limit themselves to the same industry, such as the retailing consortium based at Stirling University involving W.H. Smith, Marks and Spencer, Burton Group and Tesco.

Managers and their employers are now faced with a plethora of MBA courses from which to choose, differing in terms of curriculum, teaching methods, international flavour, relationship with the organization and, not least, cost. This bewildering choice has led to several controversial attempts to evaluate the quality of business schools' teaching and/or research.

Business school provision in the UK is not confined to the MBA. The Diploma in Management Studies (DMS) was developed in the 1950s under the auspices of the BIM and was taken over and much changed by the CNAA in the 1970s. More recently, a number of Business Schools have developed routes from certificate to diploma to masters and even to doctorate (DBA) level. A range of short courses are also provided by the business schools, aimed at all functions and levels of management. Again, these may be provided as open courses or exclusively to a particular organization.

Competency-based management development and the Management Charter Initiative (MCI)

One initiative which may reconcile the conflicting demands for professionalism in management development and the traditional British pragmatism is competency-based management development. This combines work-based assessment with formal qualifications and is formally sponsored within the Management Charter Initiative (MCI).

As we saw earlier, the MCI was launched in 1988 in response to critical reports on management education. The mission of MCI is to improve the quality of British managers through improved, more widespread and more accessible management development. It is an employer-led rather than educational-provider-driven initiative. Over a thousand employers have joined the MCI, by signing a code of practice and paying contributions based upon size.

In essence the MCI approach comprises three main elements:

- an emphasis on assessing what managers can actually do rather than what they merely know;
- a requirement for managers to compile work-based evidence to prove their competence rather than sitting examinations or writing assignments;
- the award of a management qualification on the basis of such an assessment.

The MCI is not a qualification-awarding body in itself; rather it is the lead body for the development of national standards for managers and supervisors and provides guidelines for employers, educational providers or professional bodies wishing to design their own qualification programmes, as well as encouraging awarding bodies to offer competence-based awards which incorporate the national standards. Once such programmes meet these guidelines, they are endorsed by the MCI. In 1992 there were some 15,000 managers following this qualification route and 102 MCI-accredited centres.

By 1992, occupational standards had been developed for supervisors, first-line managers and middle managers and were incorporated into the National Vocational Qualifications (NVQ) framework at levels 3, 4 and 5 respectively. The development of standards for senior managers is still awaited. All the standards specify the competencies which managers are expected to attain, performance criteria, and a range of indicators of these.

This approach to management education has several strengths. It allows for the easier identification of management training needs, given the nature of the performance criteria. It permits a flexible approach to gaining a managerial qualification, which is constrained by neither time nor place, and requires no pre-entry qualifications. Furthermore, in-company programmes can be formally accredited, so that repetition and duplication can be avoided (see box 4.5).

It is often claimed that the very real fear of failure, particularly for mature managers with few qualifications, is reduced under a competency-based approach, compared to traditional examination/ assignment-based courses. The worst fate under a competency-based programme for a manager is that they are judged not yet competent. However, it is perhaps debatable whether this is indeed more traumatic for a manager than failing an examination or course assignment external to the organization.

Box 4.5   The DVLA Certificate in Management

The UK Driver and Vehicle Licensing Agency (DVLA) was one of the first civil service departments to become an Executive Agency under the British government's 'Next Steps' reforms. The DVLA employs some 3800 employees at its Swansea headquarters and 1500 other employees country-wide, of which a fifth are in management grades. The change in status demanded new business-orientated skills from DVLA's management – for example, in marketing and purchasing – and a change in focus from functional, legislation-based specialisms to general management. As a result there has been a substantially increased emphasis on management development.

The DVLA was a founder member of the MCI, and following an audit of the existing and required skills of its managerial staff, it found that there was a close match with the competencies in the MCI's Certificate-level Management 1 standards. MCI local networks were used to obtain development secondments of managers to the private sector and an MCI pilot Certificate course was launched in October 1990. The course received MCI endorsement in April 1991 and the Agency now awards the DVLA Certificate in Management to those who successfully complete it. The agency has its own panel of assessors for the programme.

The programme takes on average 18 months to complete and commences with a computer-based assessment, purchased from the MCI, through which the participants assess their own competencies against the Management 1 standards. Line managers then use the computer program to give their view of the manager's competencies, and both profiles form the basis for discussions leading to an action plan. Those competencies in which the participant scores highly can form the basis for immediate accumulation of evidence for accreditation. Areas of low competencies are developed by in-house courses, open learning, CAL and interactive video packages, coaching from line managers, and work-based development assignments. Support-groups and troubleshooters have been established to help managers work through the programme.

The DVLA feels that a number of benefits have resulted from this initiative. Managers have become more aware of the need and potential for personal development, both for themselves and for their staff. Management performance has improved at all levels, and customer service and financial management has been improved.

Following success at the Certificate level, the DVLA is developing both Diploma and Supervisor programmes. Because of gaps in its existing provision for the former, particularly in areas such as marketing, purchasing and quality management, and a training department of only 15 full- and part-time trainers, the DVLA is planning to use an external awarding body such as a university at this level.

Sources: *Times Higher Education Supplement*, 11 September 1992: 26; Industrial Relations Services 1991d.

Supporters of the MCI claim a competitive edge in recruitment and retention, because it makes the organization more attractive to work for. One personnel manager in a local authority we interviewed informed us that a reference to support for the MCI in job advertisements had increased the number of applicants for managerial posts. Other claimed advantages of the MCI approach are that it focuses attention on all managers and not just the chosen few high-fliers, and that it gives employers a very real voice in the national debate on management education, and thus contributes to closing the academic–industrial gap (Thomson 1992).

However, there are also a number of drawbacks to the MCI approach (Stewart and Hamlin 1992). On a practical level, it is expensive, time-consuming, and complex. The mass of documentation is off-putting to managers, and assessment appears to dominate over learning. The approach also fails to accommodate a large number of specialist managers, as the occupational standards used are based upon a generalist model of management activity. Furthermore, any attempt to define management competencies that are applicable across all employers and sectors at anything other than very basic levels must in itself be highly questionable. Perhaps most damning of all is the suggestion that the MCI approach would produce inward-looking managers, rather than managers with an awareness of the changing business environment. Many organizations have in fact chosen to develop their own competencies approach, rather than use the MCI model (*Personnel Management Plus*, November 1992: 1).

The competency approach in general, and not just that of the MCI, has been criticized for a mechanical conceptualization of management, viewing managers as using a set of tools, drawn one at a time from the managerial competency tool bag. The problem of how managers re-integrate the separate competencies into a holistic performance is not addressed (Burgoyne 1989). The key question here is can a manager who has been identified as having separate managerial competencies be guaranteed to be able to use them effectively? Those critical of the approach suggest not.

Developing the international manager

Markets and organizations are internationalizing rapidly, and there is a growing need for managers with an international outlook. However, such managers are in short supply. For example, a survey of 440 European firms suggested that a shortage of international managers was the greatest factor limiting expansion abroad, and recent research finds this problem to be particularly acute for British firms (Scullion 1992a).

International experience on the part of the manager can be acquired by organizations in three main ways (Bain 1992). Firstly, companies can buy in international talent. However, as we have seen, such individuals are comparatively rare. Secondly, international expertise can be developed internally by overseas postings. This method is effective, but is slow and produces managers with experience of only a single organization. The third method, which can provide the required breadth, is through concentrated training and experience. Here, the university business schools have something to offer, with international faculty, students and ideas. Business schools around the world are generally becoming more international in their outlook and are giving greater emphasis to languages.

Developing international managers gives rise to a number of problems. The style and approach to management development may be dependent upon, and closely associated with, national cultures. It may not be easy to transfer some management development techniques from the original culture to a different one. For example, the highly expressive and open techniques used in Western countries may fail in Asian countries, where such self-revealing behaviour is not encouraged and might lead to loss of 'face'.

Equally, managers in the West would be less likely than Japanese managers to respond to an induction programme which aimed to

---

Box 4.6 Management development in Japan

Management development in large Japanese enterprises is more systematic than in many Western firms. Management development begins when the graduate joins the organization. Most of the top companies attempt to recruit graduates from the top universities. At Nissan, for example, applicants have to pass an examination testing their knowledge of the Japanese economy and their proficiency in English.

Typical development programmes begin with acculturation; new trainees are taught the way things are done in the organization and are encouraged to feel proud of its achievements. In this way, they 'acquire a keen sense of shared fate with all other company members' (Holden 1990: 243). Many managers expect to remain with one organization throughout their careers, and over a period of many years they will be given experience in most major departments and functions. Promotion is on the basis of length of service as well as on merit.

Senior managers in Japanese organizations are experienced in many facets of the business; they are multi-skilled and well able to take a realistic and holistic view of the organization for the purpose of long-term planning. To acquire this wide range of expertise, managers are moved laterally into different functions throughout their careers as part of a carefully planned development programme extending until retirement.

The managers' association with the organization becomes so intimate that they cannot easily move to a competitor, who would regard their approach as inimical to its own culture. The close association is reinforced by much socializing within the organization. A complete work group may take holidays and trips together, so reinforcing the links between team members.

Management skills are rarely acquired at outside institutions and formal MBA programmes are rare in Japan. Usually, the training is undertaken in-house, although Japanese organizations do send some of their people overseas to top business schools to study for an MBA, but usually so that they can become familiar with a foreign business culture, rather than for them to learn specific management skills. Managers may also be seconded to overseas subsidiaries, so that they gain a fuller view of the company, as well as learning something about operating in a foreign culture.

Since much of the managerial training in Japan occurs on the job, senior managers are deeply involved in developing their less-experienced colleagues. Mentoring is common. Japanese managers may spend up to 30 per cent of their time educating less experienced colleagues (Holden 1990). The culture of the organization supports management development throughout the person's career, and at all levels this sort of involvement is expected, not resented as an intrusion.

acculturate them into a complete faith in their organization. In Japan, it is in the interests of managers to completely immerse themselves in the culture of the organization to perform appropriately and to maximize their promotion prospects (see box 4.6). Western managers, by contrast, typically do not expect to remain with the organization for their entire career, so it is in their interests to retain a degree of critical detachment from it.

Increasingly, multinational organizations opt to train local managers, rather than second home-country managers to an overseas posting. There is a good argument for doing this. The local manager does not face the expatriate's problems of absorbing the cultural differences, gaining a command of the language and settling his or her family in to the local scene. Local managers already understand the nuances of the local political economy and social conditions, so their training can focus more specifically on company methods and policies and on the key managerial competencies necessary for their role. From the foregoing discussion about cultural influences it follows that the methods chosen to train local managers should be informed from head office but derived from local cultural conditions.

The alternative of training a home-country manager for posting overseas is problematic. Usually, there is little time to perform this task before the posting. Thus, courses need to be short, targeted on the destination country, industry specific, and work- as well as living-related. They would also need to continue on arrival overseas and, ideally, managers' families would also be included. Further training or counselling would probably be necessary on the manager's return, especially since the return of expatriates is often fraught with difficulties (see chapter 5).

Summary and conclusions

Management training and development are likely to continue to expand under the combined pressures of increased competition, the need for flexible, competent managers, initiatives such as the MCI, and public policy on training and education. Such pressures have already led to a critical focus on the current provision. There is a growing emphasis on quality and relevance, as perceived both by the employer and by the individual.

As organizations formulate their management development policy in the context of corporate strategic plans, there is a felt need for

Box 4.7 Management development and morality: Implications for training and development

Corporate responsibility and business ethics have become prominent issues of late, not least because of the high profile of corporate scandals such as the Guinness, and Union Carbide/Bhopal affairs, the emergence of a steady stream of corporate whistle blowers, and the debate on the 'professionalization' of management and codes of practice for managers.

However, the recent debate on management competencies has arguably ignored the moral dimension of management activity. Morality does not figure in many of the menu lists of managerial competency, and reducing 'management' to a list of competencies may emphasize the technical at the expense of the ethical and moral aspects. Yet there is evidence that managers do face moral dilemmas as an everyday aspect of their work, particularly in connection with people-management issues and in relationships with colleagues (Toffler 1986).

A number of approaches to facilitate managers' moral development are recommended. Firstly, it should be considered as a career-long need rather than something which can be accommodated simply by a one-off course. Secondly, a manager's ability to recognize, confront and resolve moral issues necessitates not only a set of cognitive skills – in particular understanding organizational behaviour and ethical reasoning – but also a wider set of 'moral attributes', including personal and interpersonal skills and self-knowledge (Maclagan 1990).

There are implications here for management development. In taught programmes, business ethics should be integrated into the general curriculum, rather than being taught as a separate subject or latched onto a business strategy course. Maclagan and Snell (1992) suggest that case studies written from an individual manager's perspective are especially valuable. They also recommend the use of experiential/action learning and mentoring, to develop a manager's skills and self-knowledge to deal with ethical issues.

dedicated programmes rather than the general courses on offer at business schools. However, such programmes may still draw on the business schools for specialist trainers and distinctive short courses, and the in-house and consortium MBA market looks likely to grow at the expense of more traditional open MBA programmes.

One clear and welcome trend in both in-company and business

school provision is towards self- rather than trainer-directed training techniques. Within self-directed learning there has been some increase in the use of new technologies such as CAL and teleconferencing. Work-based projects and competency-based approaches are also being used more widely, and there is a growing realization that management training and development encompasses more than just traditional courses.

There is likely to be a continuing change in the role of management trainers and developers. The movement towards managers learning how to learn, and the emphasis on the need to develop managers who can respond intelligently in a changing environment regardless of the skills they have learned, have profound implications. The management trainer will increasingly act as consultant, counsellor and facilitator rather than instructor. As such, the trainer will need to have general skills, rather than being simply a specialist in a narrow subject discipline, and may need to work within a team to provide the necessary expertise.

There is some evidence that organizations are beginning to realize that it is necessary to locate management development within the organization's corporate strategy, and that appropriate management training can act as an agent of cultural and organizational change. As such, management training and development is increasingly being seen as a powerful tool, which deserves the attention of senior executives. These are welcome developments, though the evidence suggests that most organizations still have much to do.

From the point of view of the employer, we can offer the following guidelines to those responsible for management development.

- Treat management development not as a cost, but as an investment which offers valuable, if difficult to quantify, returns over the long term.
- Attempt to link a systematic training needs analysis with strategic planning at the corporate level.
- Encourage senior line managers to accept greater responsibility for the development of their more junior colleagues, rather than treating management development as purely a specialist responsibility.
- Reject the idea that management development is simply about sending managers on courses, or that it all takes place early in the career. Instead, see it as a career-long and continuous activity, and pay attention to the needs of older managers.
- Focus on the individual. Avoid the 'sheep dip' approach, whereby all managers are sent on the latest course regardless of their individual needs.

- Consider using some of the more innovative techniques, such as mentoring, coaching, personal development plans, open learning, and learning contracts. These may allow management development efforts to be more easily targeted at the individual manager.
- Consider linking management development to the achievement of formal qualifications. The practice of accrediting prior learning towards competency-based qualifications has much to recommend it here. This will help add value to the process from the point of view of the individual manager.

Further reading

A helpful guide to training and development techniques is Alan Anderson, *Successful Training Practice: A Manager's Guide to Personnel Development*, Oxford: Blackwell, 1992. More specialist texts on management development are: Alan Mumford, *Management Development: Strategies for Action*, London: Institute of Personnel Management, 1989; and George Boak, *Developing Managerial Competencies*, London: Pitman, 1991.

5

Managing Managerial Careers

A career can be seen as a sequence of work activities and positions, and associated attitudes and reactions, experienced over an individual's life (Hall 1976). Whilst some now take a broader view of careers, including work and non-work commitments, our primary focus is on careers in work organizations and, more specifically, on their management. In this chapter, we show how managerial careers are being influenced by environmental and organizational change, and by corporate strategy, and we examine approaches to the management of careers.

The changing managerial career

In recent years, organizations have faced considerable change. In the private sector, competition has forced firms to look critically at their performance. Many have decided that to enable them to adapt to rapid changes in their product markets, they must adopt more flexible employment policies. The need for flexibility and innovation has led to more decentralized structures and more participative management styles. Public-sector organizations have also been under pressure, with tight control of public expenditure and more demanding governments and customers.

All this has implications for managerial careers. Moves towards greater flexibility of work organizations has often involved fewer layers of management, so that in many organizations there are fewer managerial jobs (see chapter 1). Traditional career paths are undermined, as such structures offer less predictable career ladders than more traditional bureaucratic organizations. Box 5.1 provides an

Box 5.1 Graduate recruitment and career structures in chartered accountancy

By the early 1990s, chartered accountancy firms were concerned at their inability to maintain the previous level of career opportunities. The 1980s had seen unprecedented levels of graduate recruitment by accountancy firms, who at their peak were recruiting up to 10 per cent of all graduates.

A relatively buoyant economy in the late 1980s meant that the demand for audit and other services was strong, whilst rapid expansion in the financial services sector meant that many newly qualified staff left for jobs elsewhere, providing good career opportunities for those remaining. In the early 1990s, the recession had changed all this, and the larger accountancy firms reduced their graduate recruitment by around a quarter in 1991 and 1992, whilst staff turnover declined as there were fewer jobs elsewhere. Redundancies and rationalization were widespread, partly due to the large number of mergers in the late 1980s.

However, the feeling in the profession was that such developments were more than simply a short-term adjustment. The rapid growth in financial services experienced in the 1980s was unlikely to be repeated, so that staff turnover was likely to remain low. Audit clients were becoming more sensitive about fees, and the approach to auditing was becoming more strategic, with greater use of technology. This meant that there was less of a need for large numbers of junior audit staff, and more of an emphasis on using experienced, qualified staff in a more selective way. Graduate recruitment was therefore unlikely to return to the levels of the late 1980s.

The suggestion was that the traditional pyramidical structure, with large numbers of recent graduate recruits performing the basic audit tasks and leaving for jobs in industry once qualified, was likely to change to a more rectangular form. Chartered accountancy firms would become much more selective about recruitment, in some cases recruiting directly into specialisms such as tax, management accounting and actuarial science, and perhaps even adopting a more tiered approach, with fast-track schemes for the most able.

Source: *Financial Times*, 16 April 1992: 12; and interviews with accountancy staff.

example of the impact of environmental change on early careers in one particular profession.

For the post-war 'baby-boomers' reaching middle age, promotion bottlenecks are likely, not least because of the large numbers of staff in this age group. Even new graduates are unlikely to enjoy the rapid rate of promotion experienced by the previous generation. There will be a mismatch between expectation and reality for these groups, to which organizations will need to respond if demotivation is to be avoided.

For many, not only have promotion prospects declined, but so has job security. We saw earlier how many firms made managers redundant in the recession of the early 1990s, and how managerial unemployment had increased. Such developments were not limited to this particular recession, nor indeed to the UK.

Along with mergers, takeovers and downsizing, there has been a trend towards a 'just-in-time' or numerically flexible workforce. The quest for numerical flexibility is not restricted to junior or blue-collar jobs; technical and professional specialists are increasingly being hired on a temporary or consultancy basis. Organizations can even hire managerial expertise on a short-term basis through employment agencies: so-called 'interim management' or 'executive leasing' (see below).

Even where managers are employed on standard contracts, those with portable skills are developing their careers by moving employer, perceiving advancement in terms of new challenges and higher pay, rather than in conventional promotional terms. More employers are seeking managers with experience in other organizations and industries, and there has been an increasing tendency for managers to move between employers (Alban-Metcalfe and Nicholson 1984; Mansfield and Poole 1991).

British managers have been more likely than Americans to pursue a career within their own specialities, and many British organizations have had a rigid functional structure, with little cross-fertilization at the middle-management level. However, this now appears to be breaking down, and a recent BIM survey suggested that only 21 per cent of managers had not changed function during the previous ten years (Coe and Stark 1991: 4). The finance, personnel and administration functions appear to have the more specialist career patterns.

Mobility, especially early in a person's career, appears to be important for managerial success. Those who pursue a highly specialized career may find it difficult to move into general management. Successful managers benefit from knowledge of different functions and different industries. The tendency towards greater job mobility is likely to continue as more organizations open their senior positions to external recruitment.

However, in spite of the benefits of a degree of mobility for the individual, organizations will wish to retain their most effective managers. The developments described above have implications for retention and motivation. Different forms of rewards have been used by organizations trying to motivate and retain their best people at a time of reduced promotion opportunities (see chapter 6), and rotation, intra-organizational mobility, secondments, transfers and overseas assignments have also been used. Kanter (1990) describes the post-entrepreneurial organization, where venture units allow entrepreneurial managers to run their own businesses. These, while giving employees considerable autonomy, allow the employer to offer rewards related to the economic returns to the organization.

Many of these developments demand not only movement between jobs but also geographical mobility. However, the growing number of women in the managerial workforce and the growth of dual-career families may present specific issues for the organization to address (see chapter 7).

Managing the managerial career has become central to the achievement of organizational objectives. Organizations need to retain a core of flexible managers able to learn new skills and to adjust to continuously changing jobs, yet content to remain with the organization without its necessarily being able to deliver a conventional promotional ladder. In an increasingly complex and changing world, it is more important than ever for organizations to adopt a strategic approach to the management of managerial careers.

Conventional career systems have traditionally been concerned with recruitment and selection, training and development, succession planning, promotions and exiting, including retirement, layoffs, and dismissals. Organizations may also need to provide career counselling and development programmes to help their managers with career choices and encourage them towards career decisions which benefit the organization. Such systems need close linkages with the broader corporate strategy if the supply of suitable people is to meet the demands of the organization.

However, in a recent survey of around 350 middle managers, over two-thirds felt that their employer paid insufficient attention to the management and development of their careers, whilst a survey of almost 250 organizations found that fewer than half had formal systems for identifying senior management potential (ER Consultants 1992). Whilst most organizations have formal appraisal systems, in recent years these have become increasingly preoccupied with the management of current performance rather than with career development. All this suggests that many organizations could do more to manage the career development of their managers.

Strategy and structure: Implications for career management

We argued in the introductory chapter that organizations need to match their HR strategy to their corporate strategy. Using Miles and Snow's (1978) classification of organizations into the four strategic types of defender, prospector, analyser and reactor, we showed how an organization's corporate strategy has implications for HRM. Box 5.2 sets out the implications for career management in more detail.

Given the emphasis on cost-efficiency in a stable market, the appropriate career system for *defenders* is the structured internal labour market, with recruitment at an early age, and subsequent development and promotion from within on the basis of seniority.

Box 5.2   Organizational structure, strategic orientation and career systems

	Strategic mission		
Defenders	*Analysers*	*Prospectors*	*Reactors*
Organizational structure			
Machine bureaucracy	Professional bureaucracy, adhocracy or Theory Z	Adhocracy or matrix	Inappropriate structure
Career system priority			
Retention Firm-specific functional specialists	Development Firm-specific generalists & specialists	Recruitment Independent specialists	Retrenchment Turnaround expertise & flexible generalists

| | Strategic mission | | |
Defenders	*Analysers*	*Prospectors*	*Reactors*
Managerial labour supply flow			
Early career entry	Early career entry	Entry throughout career stages	Entry limited to turnaround periods and to cheap replacement
Exit at retirement	Exit at retirement	Exit through poor individual performance or pull of outside opportunities	Exit through poor corporate performance: layoffs, dismissals, early retirements
Promotion			
Corporate service	Internal tournament	Internal & external	Little opportunity
Advance by age grading	Advance through job ladders	Contest for advancement	Survival under stress
Training and development			
Unfocused training	Appropriate retraining with job changes	Little training due to portability of skill	No training due to high turnover and financial hardship

Source: Adapted from Sonnenfeld and Peiperl 1989: 73.

Careers tend to be based on a functional specialism, and Olin and Rynes (1984) contend that the emphasis will be on the finance and production functions, given the importance of cost-efficiency. The defender organization is hierarchical, with centralized control, similar to Mintzberg's (1983) 'machine bureaucracy', where most jobs are highly standardized.

At the other extreme, the *prospector* seeks flexibility in pursuit of market opportunities, and is more likely to recruit specialists from outside, according to changing activities and requirements. Jobs are open to internal and external candidates, on the basis of merit. The appropriate structure approximates to Mintzberg's (1983) 'adhocracy', where specialists come together in multi-disciplinary teams for the duration of a specific project, and where the functional distinctions between staff and line become blurred.

Some prospectors may opt for a matrix structure, where employees have two lines of communication and control: a functional line and a product line. This shared authority allows the organization to co-ordinate complex interdependent activities without losing flexibility, and to use its specialist resources economically, because they are not confined to a single department. However, some managers dislike the ambiguity that arises, arguing that matrix structures may induce inefficiency and confusion about lines of authority.

The *analyser* is in some respects in an intermediate position. Analysers have a broader range of activities than defenders, and yet are slower to exploit new opportunities than prospectors. Early recruitment and internal development are appropriate strategies here, but with more emphasis on promotion according to merit rather than seniority, and with appropriate training as job requirements change. Analysers resemble Mintzberg's (1983) 'professional bureaucracy'. Their structure is essentially bureaucratic, but gives its specialists and professionals considerable autonomy. There may be parallel organizational hierarchies: a machine bureaucracy for the support staff and a more democratic structure for the professional staff. Such organizations may be both functionally efficient and responsive to the market, though the professional specialization and autonomy allowed may limit the speed of response to new challenges.

Reactors are organizations which lack clear strategic direction, and which have therefore failed to match their structure to a strategic mission. They are in consequence often preoccupied with retrenchment. Training, development and promotion opportunities are limited due to the emphasis on short-term crisis management and survival. Career development is likely to be limited.

Much of the recent popular management literature refers to organizations becoming more flexible, with strategies and structures approximating to those of an adhocracy (see, for example, Peters and Waterman 1982; Kanter 1990). As we have seen, environmental change is pushing many organizations in this direction, as markets become more competitive and there is a need to become more responsive to changing customer/client needs. Thus, the challenge facing many erstwhile 'defenders', who have seen their entrenched position undermined, is to successfully manage the transition to an 'analyser' or 'prospector' strategy (Herriot and Pinder 1992). This implies that the seniority-based internal labour market, with clear functional demarcations, is likely to become less widespread, with a stronger focus on strategic management development or external recruitment. Those organizations which fail to adapt to a changing environment are likely to underperform, leading ultimately to retrenchment.

This analysis allows us to make sense of both change and continuing diversity in career management. To the extent that organizations vary according to the above typology, the strategy–structure debate suggests that there is no one ideal approach to career management, but rather that the task facing organizations is to match their approach to their particular corporate strategy.

Gratton and Syrett (1990) suggest that there is also a need to recognize wider trends in the labour market, in the number of women managers and possible changes in social values which may influence attitudes to careers. Thus, in developing a career management policy, HRM specialists should scan the internal environment, particularly in terms of strategies and existing personnel and career management systems, and the broader labour market and social context. There are some planning tools which allow HRM specialists to analyse the prevailing personnel situation and predict possible future scenarios. Some of these tools are discussed below.

Human resource planning

Traditional human resource planning implies some form of matching process: between job function and job holder performance, and between demand for and supply of people. A job description is drafted in an attempt to specify the nature and content of the job, which is then converted into a person specification for the job holder and matched against the qualifications and experience of the individuals. This matching has traditionally been done in terms of the knowledge, skills and attitudes required of the job holder, though in recent years some organizations have used managerial competencies.

Careers within an organization are influenced by the range of the organization's activities. In cases such as banks or large retailers with multiple sub-units (branches and/or regions) containing similar jobs, there is often an available pool of internal candidates with the appropriate skills and experience to fill mainstream vacancies. Career paths for some managers at least may involve a relatively predictable sequence of job moves, involving progressively larger branches, for example.

Where the organization's structure is not based around such multiple units, and the range of activities and jobs is more diverse, there is a greater likelihood of moves into jobs which demand radically different skills. This implies, of course, that career planning is likely to be rather more complex in an organization with a diverse range of products or activities.

The complexity of organizations may lead to intricate career paths. There is often more than one route to the senior positions, and an individual's career path may involve a combination of horizontal and vertical moves. Lateral cross-functional moves in particular may result in multi-skilled managers with a broad view of the organization, but such movement only works without resistance and stress if the managers concerned understand and are committed to the idea that not all moves need to be vertical to be successful.

A simple but powerful way to analyse career structures in an organization is through a box-flow model. Here, all groups of staff that are linked by possible career moves are regarded as part of a personnel system. This can be depicted diagrammatically, as shown in box 5.3. Even the process of drawing such a chart can have beneficial effects. Managers' perceptions of career paths and processes can be checked against the data held by the organization on actual recruitment, promotions and departures. This can help to dispel myths and establish a more realistic view of possible career paths.

Given data on staff numbers by age and grade, along with expected levels of recruitment, promotion and wastage, the box-flow model can be used to project changes in the employment structure and in the average age of promotion, and to assess the effect of changes in the system over time. Career blockages and shortages of experienced staff can be anticipated, allowing necessary adjustments to be made in advance. Such models are best handled by computer, particularly where large and complex systems are concerned. Proprietary software is available; for example, the 'Sussex' program developed by the Institute of Manpower Studies enables the user to perform sophisticated forecasts and 'what-if' analyses of career flows, workforce structures and age profiles. However, much can be achieved with relatively simple models and standard spreadsheet packages (Malloch 1988).

Armed with forecasts of internal labour supply and career pro-

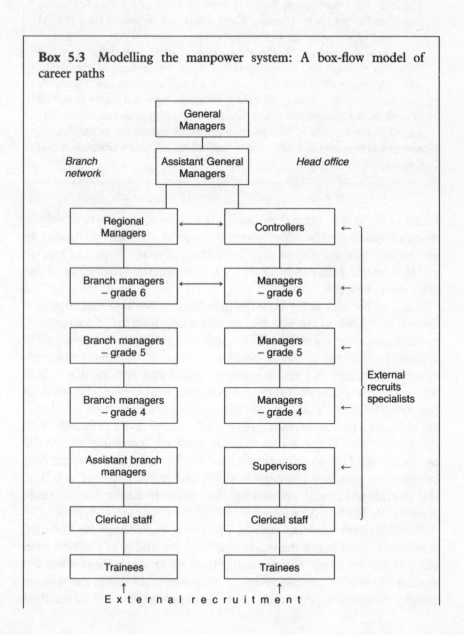

Box 5.3 Modelling the manpower system: A box-flow model of career paths

In simplified form, the manpower system of a retail financial services organization might look something like the above flow diagram.

Most staff are recruited as trainees, thereafter being promoted internally. There is little or no external recruitment into more senior grades in the branch network, although there is some external recruitment of people with specialist professional skills into head office. There is little movement between jobs in head office and branches, except at the very senior levels, where a number of people have moved into head office from the branch network.

Such a description of the manpower system represents a broad summary of flows within an organization, as experienced in the recent past. The diagram is best drawn up by a small group of line managers and personnel specialists, including someone who is directly involved in each of the main areas being mapped. The aim is to summarize the underlying structure of human resource flows within the organization, and not necessarily to reflect every individual job move (Bennison and Casson 1984).

gression from the human resource model, with forecasts of labour demand based on the organization's business strategic plan, and an analysis of wastage and of trends in the external labour market, an HRM strategic plan can be drawn up. A schematic illustration of this is given in box 5.4.

Such a plan may show how the matching of demand and supply of labour is to be achieved: by recruitment, internal development, redundancies or transfers. The methods chosen will have implications for human resource policies, including training and development programmes, performance appraisal and remuneration. It is vital that the planning exercise feeds into action plans for each of the key HR functions. All too often, organizations have produced sophisticated human resource plans, only to see them gather dust on the shelf. The emphasis in human resource planning should be on involving HR and line managers in the collection and analysis of data, on producing analyses which are relevant to the needs of the organization, and on making the analysis intelligible to those responsible for key decisions.

However, such human resource planning techniques are not used universally, and many managers question the utility of detailed forecasts in an uncertain environment. Interest in these approaches has fluctuated, often declining in use in response to economic pressure to reduce manpower, cut costs and raise productivity. Longer-term

Box 5.4   Human resource planning: An overview

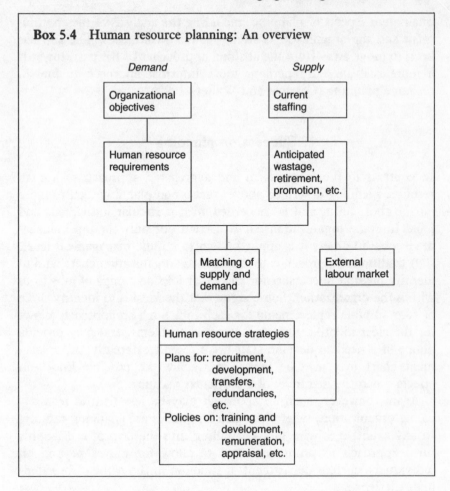

vision often returns as the economy recovers, particularly when skills shortages emerge.

Furthermore, this approach may pose problems for organizations faced with rapid change and the need to adapt quickly. The process concentrates on the current job, not on future skills needs, and it does not easily accommodate the idea of in-job development because of its fixation on matching. The approach appears more suited to a mature, stable bureaucracy, rather than to the flexible, fast-changing organization which is increasingly seen as appropriate in many sectors.

In recent years, human resource planning has begun to place less emphasis on detailed mathematical models, giving more attention to

qualitative aspects of planning, including the analysis of the environment and the organization's strengths and weaknesses. The aim has
been to move away from the abstract approaches of the past, towards
a more relevant, and perhaps more informal approach to human
resource planning (Cowling and Walters 1990).

Succession planning

In contrast to the longer-term and aggregated approach to human
resource planning described above, succession planning focuses more
on the short term, and is concerned with particular individuals and
jobs. In some organizations, it is carried out only for top management jobs; in others it is applied down to middle-management level.

A traditional approach is to examine the organization chart, and to
identify possible successors for particular jobs or groups of jobs from
within the organization. Some argue that the ideal is to identify three
or four suitable replacements for each job. Such an approach allows
for the clear identification of succession problems, and may provide
notice of a need to develop staff or to recruit externally. A replace-
ment chart may also be useful in tracing the possible knock-on
effects down the hierarchy of a particular vacancy.

Again, however, such an approach may be less fruitful in a dynamic organization, where jobs and structures are changing rapidly.
In any event, it is wise to avoid falling into the trap of a 'Buggin's
turn' approach to promotion, and to allow for moves beyond an
individual's current department or function in the name of broaden-
ing experience.

Of course, even where suitable successors have been identified
through succession planning, this need not mean that the short list is
restricted to such individuals. Succession planning is not necessarily
inconsistent with an open promotion policy. Indeed, in a sense the
major benefit comes not when succession planning identifies a particular candidate, but rather where it gives forewarning of a possible
succession problem, and allows corrective action to be taken.

There is some evidence of a growing sophistication in succession
planning. Many organizations are now going beyond the traditional
'one step' approach of identifying possible successors to a limited
range of senior management posts, by drawing up development
plans for potential senior managers early in their careers. As Hirsh
puts it:

This change in scope implies a change in underlying objectives. Succession planning is now less concerned with short-term post filling and more concerned with the proactive development of the senior managers of the future. (1990: 2)

The succession planning process is now likely to involve a group of senior managers drawn from a range of functions, meeting as a succession or management development committee. This may give the development process a broader perspective, recognizing the value of cross-functional moves as part of career development. Succession planning is also making greater use of systematic analyses of competency profiles in planning management development.

Assessing individual potential and development needs

All this leaves unanswered a critical question: where do we get the information needed to make judgements about individual potential and development needs? A common approach is that performance appraisal is used to provide information on both past performance and on potential. Appraisal may be seen as an integral part of the development process, resulting in a career development plan for the individual manager. Our own research suggests, however, that this is the aspect of appraisal which managers tend to be least happy about (see chapter 3). It is not surprising, then, that those responsible for managerial career planning often draw on additional sources of information.

Assessment centres have been used by many organizations as an aid to management development. This involves the assessment of a small, selected group of candidates by a team of judges on the basis of their performance in a comprehensive and integrated series of exercises, which may represent job-related tasks and problems. Usually, an assessment centre evaluates candidates against eight to twelve managerial competencies, such as planning, problem analysis, interpersonal awareness, and persuasiveness. Typical exercises include the 'in-tray', in which the candidate has to respond to ten to fifteen written items in a limited time period, leaderless group discussions, case studies, pen and paper tests, questionnaires, role-plays and interviews.

Assessment centres tend to be used mainly for developmental and promotion purposes amongst junior and middle management ranks, and for selecting graduates on management training programmes (see chapter 4). Interest in assessment centres appears to be growing. In the UK, organizations such as Cadbury, Lloyds Bank, Norwich Union, J. Sainsbury, STC, the Wellcome Foundation, Glaxo, and Rover use assessment centres for managerial positions, though they appear to be used less often in the public sector (Industrial Relations Services 1991a).

By tracing the subsequent promotion of participants, Howard (1974) concluded that assessment centres show high predictive validity. However, there are drawbacks with the technique. Those not selected to participate in the programme may feel that their development needs are being neglected, relative to the 'high fliers'. Those who do not perform well may feel that their future with the organization is blighted, when in fact they may be performing their current job well. There is a fear that the stress inherent in the concentration of testing could cause some to underperform.

The success of an assessment centre depends on the quality of the assessors. Assessors must themselves be properly trained to perform this role, so that time demands may be quite significant. Senior managers are the obvious choice as assessors, but these people are often the least likely to spare sufficient time. Many companies hire consultant psychologists to help them to design a suitable assessment programme and train the assessors.

The provision of feedback to participants on the outcomes of the assessment raises a number of issues. It is difficult to balance the need for truthful reporting on performance and potential with the need to avoid demotivating the participant. In Dulewicz's (1991) longitudinal survey at STC Telecommunications, a quarter of participants said they wanted more frank, detailed and constructive feedback. However, some general managers had vetoed frank discussion for fear of discouraging or losing valued staff. The same survey suggested that the recommendations arising out of the assessment centre were often not implemented, though it appeared that recommendations for training were more likely to be implemented than those relating to job changes. Furthermore, of the 20 participants who had left the company after four years, 11 had been assessed as having high potential.

Since a major drawback of assessment centres is their cost, not least in the time of senior managers, it would be ironic if those assessed as having the greatest potential were subsequently to leave the organization. In order to retain such people, it is important that any recommendations are properly implemented and follow-up action taken. Mentors drawn from senior management can be valuable here, and can provide regular counselling and advice (see chapter 4).

The assessment centre's potential for unfair discrimination has attracted increasing attention. Whilst studies have found little gender discrimination in assessment centres (Iles 1989; Alban-Metcalfe 1989), a number of concerns remain, in particular that the identification of criteria for job success tends to be derived from a predominantly male group. Given the increasing use of assessment centres, there have been calls for the Institute of Personnel Management and the British Psychological Society to issue a code of practice and for the formation of a group of users, designers and suppliers to ensure that a minimum set of standards prevails and some form of quality control is developed (Blanksby and Iles 1990).

Career development programmes: Matching organizational and individual needs

Promotion policies can be either closed or open. In the former, fast-trackers are selected for special attention, and may be afforded privileged access to promotion opportunities. The advantage of such an approach is that development efforts can be targeted and succession planning made easier. However, closed promotion policies also have several disadvantages. Fast-trackers may be given experience of many different functions in very little time, often insufficient to fully master the skills inherent in the job or to receive feedback on work performance. Other individuals in the organization may feel envious towards this special group and feel demotivated. Closed promotion systems have also aroused concern on equal opportunities grounds, with the fear that they may discriminate against women and minorities (see chapter 7).

In open promotion policies, employees are informed about their own potential and their possible career paths, and anyone can apply for jobs as they are advertised. For an open promotion policy to function properly, information about opportunities must be widely available and individuals must be given the opportunity to develop their skills. To achieve this, increasing numbers of organizations are offering career development programmes to their managers.

Schein argues that an ideal human resource planning and development system attempts to reconcile the organization's need for suitable staffing with the individual's need for 'personal career growth and development' (1987: 30). A major tool in effecting this reconciliation is individual career counselling, within a well-structured career development programme. It is vital that such a programme is based on an understanding of individual needs. We begin by considering individual career choice.

Holland (1973) takes a psychological perspective on career choice, based upon personality differences. He argues that people will seek to work in an environment which matches their personality type. For example, those of the 'investigative' personality type are said to have an 'analytical and curious' orientation, and so are likely to choose such careers as research and development or engineering. In contrast, individuals of the 'social' personality type are said to have a 'training and helping' orientation, and so tend to choose careers such as education, social work or counselling.

However, such theories have been strongly criticized, not least because they focus on career intentions rather then on actual choices (Nicholson 1987). It is important to recognize that many people do not exercise an unconstrained choice of career; rather they were 'in the right place at the right time' (Bamber 1986). Careers are often a series of almost accidental or opportunistic decisions (Nicholson and West 1988). Some evidence suggests that people may change their aspirations to fit the job more readily than the reverse, thus casting doubt on the role of personality types in determining career choice.

Some theorists argue that just as people develop throughout their lives, so they also develop a concept of self with regard to their careers. If we accept that people move through predictable stages of adaptation to their careers:

> then identifying the patterns and issues associated with various ages and stages may help our understanding of individuals' attitudes and behaviors in organizations. From a human resource and managerial perspective, this understanding may allow for more effective organizational career planning programs . . . (Ornstein et al. 1989: 117)

According to Super's (1957) career stage development model, individuals move through four career stages: trial, establishment, maintenance and decline. The key psychological tasks facing the individual at each stage are:

- *Trial* Individuals are concerned to explore their interests and capabilities, and to identify their professional self-image.
- *Establishment* Individuals become strongly committed to their chosen career and are preoccupied with career advancement.
- *Maintenance* The priority is to hold on to what has been achieved.
- *Decline* Individuals become less preoccupied with their career, and seek an alternative self-image which is independent of career success.

Levinson's life stage development model relates this more closely to the life cycle (see box 5.5). Both models emphasize that an individual's needs, and hence their attitudes and behaviour, are likely to change over time. The argument is that individuals have many goals and interests in life, but that only a subset of these will be of primary concern at any one time.

Ornstein et al. (1989) have attempted to test the two models. In their research, they adopted various measures to assess the career stage, career attitudes, job attitudes, job satisfaction, organizational commitment and performance of 535 sales people. From their survey data they deduced that both Levinson's and Super's models were largely supported during the early stages of people's careers. Thus, those 'in the trial stages of their careers were less committed, satisfied, involved, and challenged by their jobs' (1989: 131). However, those in the decline stage did not express greater job dissatisfaction or reduced commitment to their work, as Super's theory predicts. It would be worth repeating this research with a sample of managers.

The recognition of such a career life cycle is critical in designing a career-management strategy. In the early stages, the key concern is to develop basic job skills and to allow individuals to discover their own preferences and how they fit into the organization (Evans 1986). Since the new recruit is passing through a phase of 'reality testing', the first impression may be crucial in socializing the individual into the organization. Realistic recruiting may help here, and the recruiter needs to avoid overselling the organization and should give a reasonable view of the recruit's possible career paths (see chapter 2).

Kotter (1990) maintains that challenge early in a career is most important in producing good leaders, and he argues that this is easier to offer in a decentralized organization, since responsibility is sited lower in the hierarchy. Exposure to the right sort of challenge helps the individual establish what Schein (1978) calls the 'career anchor': the dominant career concern which the individual will conserve

Box 5.5 Levinson's life stage development model

Life stage (age)	Tasks to be accomplished
Early adulthood (20–40)	
Early adult transition (17–22)	To begin thinking about one's place in the world separate from the institutions of youth (such as parents, school). To test one's initial choices about preferences for adult living.
Entering the adult world (23–28)	To develop a sense of personal identity in the world of work and non-work (such as family, community).
Thirties transition (29–33)	To evaluate accomplishments of the 20s and make adjustments to the life structure adopted.
Settling down (34–39)	To strive towards achievement of personal and professional goals. To make strong commitments to work, family and community.
Middle adulthood (40–60)	
Mid-life transition (40–45)	To review life structure adopted in the 30s. To recognize mortality and limits on achievements and answer the questions raised by these issues.
Entering middle adulthood (46–50)	To develop greater stability as answers to questions posed in earlier stage are incorporated into mindset.
Fifties transition (51–55)	To raise questions about life structure previously adopted.
Culmination of middle adulthood (56–60)	To answer questions previously raised and adjusted to life choices.

Source: Suzyn Ornstein, William L. Cron and John W. Slocum, Life stage versus career stage: A comparative test of the theories of Levinson and Super. *Journal of Organizational Behavior*, 10, 2, April, 1989, pages 117–34. Copyright 1989 John Wiley and Sons Ltd. Reprinted by permission of John Wiley and Sons, Ltd.

whenever a choice has to be made. He identifies five career anchors:

- *Technical/Functional* People with this career anchor prefer to remain in their chosen functional area and reject general management opportunities.
- *Managerial competence* People with this career anchor are strongly motivated to become managers and believe that they have the analytical, interpersonal and emotional competence to rise to this level.
- *Creativity* Those with a career anchor of creativity are often successful entrepreneurs, fulfilling an inner need to create something that reflects themselves alone.
- *Autonomy and independence* Such a career anchor is held by those who abhor the large organization. They often have a technical/functional leaning which, combined with their desire for autonomy, leads them to act as consultants or professionals.
- *Security* Long-term job security is the prime concern of this group, who will passively accept the careers meted out to them by the organization as long as stability is maintained.

Individuals develop their career anchor during the early stages of their career, often on the basis of early experience. The individual will not necessarily always be performing work which is consistent with their career anchor, but once formed, it serves as a reference point for career decisions. Ideally, modern career management aims to use early job pathing creatively, to give individuals the chance to reassess and review their career anchors so that the organization benefits from managers having a broad multifunctional insight into the organization's operation.

In the middle phase of the individual's career, once the basic career anchor has been established, the priority is to achieve logical career progression. Whilst job moves every two years or so may be welcomed by younger managers keen to explore their career interests, by this stage such frequent moves may no longer be necessary. Indeed, the manager may now face greater demands from family and domestic life, so that a job move every four or five years is likely to be more appropriate. Similarly, training needs will have moved on from basic skills to more strategic business issues (Evans 1986).

The risk in career planning and management development is that there may be a tendency to concentrate on younger staff and high fliers, to the exclusion of both older managers and solid performers (Davies and Deighan 1986; see box 5.6). For example, Warr (1993) reports a tendency for older managers to receive less training than their younger colleagues, particularly in larger organizations. Whilst

---

Box 5.6 A portfolio approach to managerial performance

Odiorne (1984) has extended the Boston Consulting Group's analysis of business strategy by using it to classify managers in portfolio form.

Workhorses are those managers who are high performers but who are of limited potential. They have now 'plateaued', because of limited ability or ambition. This group may form the majority of an organization's managerial stock. *Stars* are those managers whose current performance is high and who also have potential to move on to more challenging posts. *Problem* managers are those who have potential, but who are not performing particularly well in their current job. New entrants, for example graduate trainees, are likely to fall into this category. Given appropriate training and development, such people may develop into workhorses or stars. However, if such assistance is not forthcoming, the danger is that they may slip into the *deadwood/dog* category in time.

Odiorne (1984) argues that such a categorization may be useful in outlining a management development strategy. The use of performance appraisal is a valuable tool here, not only to aid the classification process but also to provide a platform to diagnose and organize such action. Odiorne outlines an approach suggested to him by an American manager: 'we polish the stars, fix the problems, feed the workhorses plenty of hay, and shoot the dogs'.

However, whilst the above scheme gives some food for thought, it may be that organizations have tended to follow such an approach too literally, concentrating training and development resources on the high fliers and paying insufficient attention to maintaining the commitment of the solid performers (see text).

---

organizations may need to offer early retirement, or deal with 'blockers' (poor performers, far from retirement but with little chance of promotion) in order to produce enough challenging opportunities (Kotter 1990), identifying the true 'blocker' may not be easy. Furthermore, older managers have amassed experience and knowledge which may be extremely valuable to their employer. Even the suggestion that employers receive lower returns from investing in the development of their older managers may be wrong, since older managers are less likely to leave for alternative employment (Warr 1993: 8).

When attention is focused on those with great potential, it is easy for organizations to overlook the competent manager, who would prefer new challenges irrespective of promotion. Ignored, such people are no longer given challenging assignments and can become demoralized. The prophesy of decline and poor performance is self-fulfilling, as the manager moves towards stagnation. A danger facing many organizations is that with slower growth, organizational delayering and career blockages, such problems may affect a growing proportion of managers at an earlier age (Davies and Deighan 1986).

Such managers need recognition and challenge within a steady-state career, which offers expansion rather than a ladder to climb. A flatter, perhaps matrix-style organization is particularly conducive to this. Since there are so few levels between junior and senior employees, career growth comes from expansion of the job rather than promotion. Such an approach, with its emphasis on lateral movement, may also give a broader foundation to a career.

A move away from the simple hierarchical career structure not only serves the steady-state careerist and the new recruit needing an early challenge, but also the spiralist who will follow a career path for five to seven years before spiralling off to a related career. This career spiralling results in a layered career where the individual experiences various associated areas. For example, they may move from engineering, to sales, to corporate planning, to consultancy, only to return to their first employer as a general manager with broader competencies (Evans 1990).

Dual ladders: Accommodating professionals within organizational career structures

The difficulty of accommodating professionals, and particularly technical professionals such as engineers and scientists, within organizational career structures is a long-standing one. In many organizations, if such professionals are to progress in career terms, they must leave behind their technical specialism and move into a managerial role. This may lead to a number of problems.

Firstly, some able and productive professionals are 'forced' into managerial roles in order to attain higher rewards and status. As a result of this the technical talents of the professional are lost to the organization, the reward for technical excellence is promotion into management, and the 'laboratory becomes a school for making non-scientists of its scientists' (Shepard 1958: 178).

Secondly, an associated problem with such career systems is

accommodating the technically excellent but managerially incompetent professional. There is a real danger that such individuals become demotivated due to a lack of career progression and recognition. Thirdly, given the general reduction in the available managerial posts in the 1990s, only a small number of the technically sound and managerially competent may actually make the career transformation to manager, so that retention of the remaining professionals again becomes an issue for the organization.

The dual career ladder has been developed in an attempt to deal with such problems (see box 5.7). It aims to provide professionals with career opportunities, without their necessarily moving into purely managerial jobs. Several types of dual ladder systems are in use, the most common being the parallel ladder. Here, there is a traditional hierarchy of managerial posts. In addition, however, there is a parallel 'professional' hierarchy of positions roughly equating with the managerial posts in terms of salary and status, with titles such as 'research associate', 'scientific adviser', or 'research fellow'.

Box 5.7   Dual career ladders at Eastman Chemical Company

Like many companies, Eastman's has reorganized and cut the number of managerial posts. One effect of this has been to reduce the attractiveness of a management career for its professional staff. Following these changes, concerns arose in the company about its ability to attract and retain top scientific talent. In response to this, Eastman's set up an 'Advancement Ladder Study Team' in 1988 to review its career structures.

Eastman's existing structure consisted of a parallel ladder system with separate professional and managerial ladders. Internal surveys found strong support for the view that managerial and non-managerial posts make an equal contribution to the company. Furthermore, in recent years the company has placed a greater emphasis on the need for flexibility and teamworking. The study team saw its 'goal post ladder' as a way to address these issues.

The new ladder would have a single 'upright' which contained both managerial and professional posts, as shown below in the diagram. This single ladder allowed for flexibility between managerial and purely technical jobs. At the top of the upright would be the start of a two-tier parallel ladder. At this senior level it was envisaged that transfers between the ladders would be less frequent.

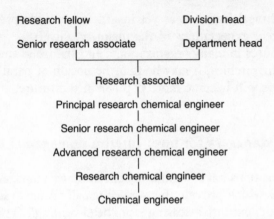

A year and a half after implementation the company again surveyed its staff to evaluate the new career system and found that in general the new structure was well-received. The exception was that there had been no improvement in the staff's evaluation of the equity and consistency of the promotion criteria. Eastman's is continuing to work on this aspect.

Source: Grant and Holmes 1991.

However, there are a number of problems with such dual systems in practice (Allen and Katz 1986). Those occupying senior technical posts may experience a lack of role definition due to the ambiguous relationship between the technical and managerial ladders. There is also a danger that such posts are seen simply as a second-class reward for long service and organizational loyalty, rather than for technical excellence. Promotion within the technical ladder may even be seen as a sign of managerial inadequacy and thus stigmatized as a convenient 'shelf' to place problem professionals. Most limiting of all for the attractiveness of the technical ladder is the lack of power and authority of such posts, compared with their managerial equivalents.

Allen and Katz (1986) surveyed some 1500 engineers and found that the managerial career track was more popular than a technical one. Similarly, Bailyn (1980) found that a very high proportion of scientists and engineers see their career goals in terms of eventual progress into management, often from the outset of their careers. Of course, such preferences may simply reflect the fact that most successful role models have hitherto moved into management, and

that the technical ladder is as yet insufficiently widespread to influence the career expectations of the majority. Given the pressures on
career structures in many organizations, and the trend towards flatter
managerial hierarchies, it may be that the notion of parallel technical
career ladders will become more popular in the future.

Managers for hire: Interim management

Some organizations have found it beneficial to use managerial 'temps'.
The agencies which provide this service usually refer to it as 'interim
management', 'executive leasing', or 'head-renting'. This approach
to resourcing managers was imported into the UK in the 1980s and
although it has been used more widely in the USA and in some
continental European countries, such as Holland, it is said to be
growing rapidly in the UK (Hogg 1989). There are no figures available on the size of the British market, but a recent report put the
number in the USA as high as 200,000 (Bogan 1990).

One of the key advantages claimed for the use of interims is that
they can be supplied quickly, within five to fifteen days. Some
organizations use interims as a stop gap, whilst a more permanent
manager is being sought. This takes the time pressure off a search
and avoids mistakes being made through undue haste. Interim managers may be used where vacancies suddenly arise due to death,
sickness or termination, or where a particular one-off need arises.
The latter include mergers, acquisitions, management buy-outs, relo-
cations, privatizations and recruitment drives. Recent examples include the leasing of 40 managers from P-E Inbucon to manage the
merger forming the UK engineering company FKI–Babcock, the
use of interims by the UK utility Anglia Water to manage its stock
market flotation, and a Dutch university that hired an interim to
assist in the downsizing of its organization (Hogg 1989).

Some have argued that a growth in the leasing of managers is
a deliberate policy decision of employers to introduce numerical
flexibility into a hitherto core group:

Charles Handy's predictions of 'clover leaf' organization structures
composed of a small nucleus of permanent managers pulling in additional help as and when required, are becoming a reality. (Hogg
1989: 134)

However, some organizations appear to be using interims instead of management consultants, rather than at the expense of permanent managers. Management consultants have been the traditional source of numerical flexibility at the management level in the UK, and we may simply be seeing the substitution of one flexible resource for another.

Relative cost may provide one explanation for the increased use of managerial leasing at the expense of consultants, with the average cost of an interim manager being a half to two-thirds lower than the average consultancy fee. Also, it is claimed that there is less distance between the client and the interim than between client and consultant. The management consultant acts as an 'off-line adviser', providing the client with possible alternative courses of action. The interim, by contrast is more involved, not only in making decisions but also in implementing them.

Compared to permanent managers, the use of interims brings savings on pension, termination and other payroll costs. According to the advertising literature of P-E Inbucon, interims also come to the organization 'free from politics and personal hang-ups' and are 'sensibly over-qualified'. Interim executives are also marketed as 'doers who are committed to succeed', 'quick learners' and 'experienced self-starters'.

However, there is a potential downside to the use of interims. They may lack understanding of the client organization's culture, and this can lead to the neglect of cultural issues in decision implementation. There may also be problems of acceptability where permanent employees report to an interim manager, particularly if the interim has to take some tough decisions. Another potential problem is the issue of confidentiality – though fears may be unfounded here, since any breach of confidentiality could amount to professional suicide for the interim, who needs to maintain a good reputation to ensure future hires.

Probably the most serious problem for managerial leasing agencies to overcome is the image of interims as out of work, unemployable managers 'resting' between real jobs. A description of American executive interims as 'basic job-seekers, . . . retirees, golden parachuters, working mothers, and career-interim executives' is a typical characterization (Bogan 1990: 10). In response to such a perception, the UK leasing industry has recently established its own trade association, the Association of Temporary and Interim Executive Services

(ATIES), in order to 'reassure the public that we are not cowboys or peddling duff consultants' (Hogg 1989: 134).

Expatriates and the 'international manager'

In the traditional multinational companies, the number of expatriate managers appears to be declining, not least because of political pressure from host countries, who are suggesting that their own nationals should hold more senior positions (Brewster 1988). However, the total number of managers who take an overseas post is likely to increase, due to greater internationalization in business, and the trend towards shorter-spell overseas assignments in place of the 'career expatriate' of the past (Scullion 1992b).

Managers may be sent overseas because local staff lack the necessary expertise to do the job; as part of the individual manager's development programme; to try to inculcate the parent organization ethos into the local organization; to start new ventures or make new contacts; or to allow the parent company to exercise closer control over its subsidiaries (Brewster 1988: 10).

Although one of the major reasons for overseas transfer is to give the manager an opportunity to grow in expertise and to benefit from a challenging experience, the experience is sometimes too challenging. Settling into a new culture is an additional stress above the normal pressures faced when starting in a new position. There are also training implications with overseas transfers (see chapter 4).

Even if the expatriate manager survives the first few months successfully and goes on to integrate well into the host culture and business environment, this is not necessarily the end of the difficulties, since the return home may be problematic. The life style in the host country and the manager's status and independence in the smaller organization often cannot be replicated in the larger home base organization, so that some managers do not wish to return (Brewster 1988).

Those who do return may have unrealistic expectations about both their home country and their potential for challenging employment there. Often, organizations make little provision for the returning manager, who may face effective demotion and demoralization. Things will have moved on while the manager has been overseas, and the repatriate may have to learn new procedures and adjust to new technologies, often without adequate preparation (Dowling and Schuler 1990).

Such difficulties may discourage some managers from accepting overseas assignments. Perhaps more importantly, repatriates finding it difficult to adjust may leave to join other, possibly rival, organizations. To avoid the loss of these experienced managers, organizations need to provide adequate training to managers and their families before they leave, to keep in close contact while they are overseas, and to anticipate their return by providing re-entry counselling support and a suitably attractive re-entry position.

In a study of the repatriation of managers in 29 UK multinationals, Johnston (1991) found that whilst most companies claimed to have some form of career development help, for example by planning for the placement of repatriates within the company, rather less was done on a personal level to assist the returning manager. Reorientation courses and counselling were offered by only a few companies. It appears that UK multinationals lack a coherent and comprehensive approach to repatriation.

This finding is all the more worrying in light of suggestions that there is a growing shortage of managers with international experience, critical in an era of growing internationalization. There is evidence that managers are becoming more reluctant to take overseas postings, because of an unwillingness to disrupt children's education and the spouse's career, and also because of concern about re-entry in a period of uncertainty. In response, UK companies are sending younger staff overseas, in some cases making a virtue of this in their graduate recruitment literature (Scullion 1992b).

Outplacement and retirement

In the early 1990s, there appeared to be less job security for managers than in the past. Many displaced managers have difficulty finding a new job of similar or higher status, especially those who have remained with the same employer for most of their career. Some of them become freelance consultants, but sometimes this is merely a facade to conceal unemployment and the attendant stigma of failure. Others start a new business, but such small businesses often fail.

To prevent such sad waste of talent and experience, some large organizations have established support arrangements for those displaced. In a survey of 148 UK organizations carried out in 1989, 81 per cent offered redundant managers an outplacement counselling service, with large organizations being more likely to provide such a service than smaller ones. The service was provided when employers were declaring redundancies (95 per cent), reorganizing or merging (77 per cent), 'for personal chemistry problems' (56 per cent), and when employees reached a career plateau (49 per cent) (*Employment Gazette*, January 1990: 49).

The London Residuary Body (LRB), faced with winding up the Greater London Council's (GLC) affairs within five years, had an in-house programme which included training in job search techniques plus the provision of a curriculum vitae typing agency, job shop and regular vacancy circular. Redundant personnel were also given advice on starting a business, working for charity, and franchising. Where their own in-house programme proved inadequate staff were referred to outplacement consultants for special help (Rayner 1992).

In recent years there has been a growth in the number of outplacement consultants offering advice and assistance with job search, help with designing curriculum vitae and developing interview skills. They also provide counselling to assist with the psychological and financial problems which may accompany job loss. Fees are usually around 15 per cent of the manager's previous annual salary, plus £1000 to £1500 (Crofts 1992). Outplacement consultants may be hired either by corporate clients, as part of a package for staff affected by redundancy, or directly by individual managers.

There has been concern about the quality of service provided by outplacement consultants, especially with the number of small firms in the industry – sometimes individuals who have themselves been made redundant. However, with the publication of an IPM code of practice on career and outplacement consultants, and with an increasing awareness amongst corporate clients of what the consultants have to offer, there is some evidence of a growing professionalism (Crofts 1992).

Counselling may also be offered to retiring managers. There has been debate that the enforced retirement of able managers is a waste of valuable expertise and experience. Some maintain that the expected decline in productivity from the older manager is largely a self-fulfilling prophecy, as people perform according to expectations. In Japan, by contrast, age is venerated as a source of accumulated wisdom and many of the top executives in the largest organizations are over the conventional Western retirement age. Lower and middle managers of large companies in Japan are expected to retire at 55 but will be introduced to a part-time opportunity with a satellite company to continue their working life for a further ten years or more (Ouchi 1981).

It may be that such an option would be preferred by UK managers. In a survey of the work and leisure attitudes of the over-40s, most wanted a flexible retirement date between 51 and 60 and preferred the chance to work part-time or on temporary assignments (KPMG Peat Marwick Management Consultants/Institute of Personnel Management 1990).

Some UK organizations are adopting such an approach, particularly where older managers are being asked to make room for the career development of younger staff. Organizations may make special arrangements to gradually ease the manager into retirement by introducing part-time working. In some cases these experienced managers have been retained as consultants. In 1990, for example, IBM set up 'Skillbase' to absorb older employees. Initially it offered a guaranteed level of work via IBM, who retained a 40 per cent interest, plus the freedom to consult for other organizations (Mayo 1991). Increasingly, the Skillbase consultants are being encouraged to find the bulk of their work outside IBM, on a commercial basis.

In most developed nations the proportion of older people in the population is growing, and with this growth might be expected some shift in political influence from the young to the old. In such circumstances the management of retirement will remain a critical issue for organizations. In the future, the declining number of young people may mean that the emphasis shifts towards attracting and retaining mature staff, leading to a conflict of interest with those who wish to retire early.

Summary and conclusions

Labour market and demographic trends are encouraging organizations to rethink their approach to the management of careers, and increasing competition has made them more aware of the need for strategic planning. Where organizations have decided on a flexible response to the challenges of the 1990s, they may adopt a less hierarchical structure. As competition remains intense, as technological change proceeds, and as the pressure for change in the public sector continues, this flexible response may well become more widespread.

These developments have implications for organizations and for managers themselves:

- Many organizations will need to become increasingly reliant on the external recruitment of those with specific professional skills.
- Where there is a continued emphasis on the internal development of managers, a flatter hierarchy and the consequent reduction in promotion opportunities mean that there will be a need to think in terms of more flexible career paths. Career-development strategies should encourage managers to expand their experience and knowledge by taking advantage of appropriate alternatives to promotion, such as transfers, secondments, job rotation, overseas experience and entrepreneurial experience, all supported by an emphasis on continuing training and development.
- In many cases, promotion can no longer be relied upon as the primary reward for good performance, so there will be a need to look for other forms of reward. Managers need to be developed and motivated effectively within a given job, with obvious implications for remuneration strategies and other aspects of HRM.
- Managers themselves need to think about their careers as possibly involving more than the ascent of a particular organizational hierarchy. They need to think in terms of growth within their current job, of lateral, perhaps cross-functional, moves, and of moves to other organizations. Managers will have to take greater responsibility for their own career development.

However, we have found that in practice formal succession planning is often lacking and that, increasingly, appraisal tends to be preoccupied with the management of current performance. Many managers are concerned about the lack of promotion opportunities and feel that their organizations could do more to help them develop their careers. Whilst all this may be taken as being consistent with a strategy of external recruitment rather than internal development, there appears to be an element of short-termism in the approach of some employers. For many organizations, the challenge of the 1990s and beyond will still be to combine the management of current performance with a longer-term development perspective.

Further reading

Those seeking a more detailed treatment of approaches to career management are referred to the book by Andrew Mayo, *Managing Careers: Strategies for Organizations*, London: Institute of Personnel Management, 1991. A more detailed treatment of the techniques of human resource planning is to be found in Malcolm Bennison and Jonathan Casson, *The Manpower Planning Handbook*, London: McGraw-Hill, 1984.

6

Remuneration and the Manager

There has been a growing emphasis on the view that remuneration can be used as a strategic management tool, not only to recruit, retain and motivate, but also to manage corporate performance and to influence corporate values and beliefs (Curnow 1986; Incomes Data Services 1990b; Armstrong and Murlis 1991). This is consistent with the notion that personnel policies and practices should support corporate objectives. In this sense, remuneration policies should be driven by strategic choices.

However, such strategic choices are influenced by a changing corporate environment. Recent years have seen significant political developments in the UK. Successive Budgets have altered the relative tax efficiency of various forms of remuneration, notably by cutting income tax, taxing fringe benefits more heavily, and providing fiscal incentives for share ownership. Privatization and the promotion of more entrepreneurial styles of management in the public sector, and the encouragement of an 'enterprise culture' have had a major impact on remuneration policies.

The economic context is also important. Lower levels of inflation provide greater scope for the individualization of annual pay increases, as general cost of living pay rises become less significant. Skills shortages lie behind many of the innovations in remuneration policies, particularly in the South-east of England during the late 1980s. Developments in product markets are also important, with an intensification of international competition, product development, new technology, privatization, deregulation and competitive restructuring all requiring a response from organizations in terms of greater efficiency and improved performance and quality.

Such political and economic developments have two key implications for remuneration policy. Firstly, they remove many of the obstacles to the strategic use of remuneration. The tax changes and the lower levels of inflation, for example, give organizations more scope to experiment with cash pay. Secondly, they place new demands on organizations and their managers, often requiring greater effectiveness and responsiveness to customers. Remuneration policy has increasingly been seen as a key management tool in meeting such demands.

In this chapter, we examine the ways in which organizations reward their managers, and show how remuneration strategies are developing. We begin with a review of the factors likely to influence an organization's remuneration strategy. We then go on to discuss the changing role of job evaluation, the development of performance-related rewards, the role of benefits, and the increasing use of personal contracts.

Remuneration policy: A strategic perspective

Management remuneration is influenced by a variety of factors. Chief amongst these are the responsibilities or 'size' of the job, the characteristics of the individual job holder, labour market conditions, the state of the product market, and the employer's remuneration philosophy (see box 6.1).

Job size has been the main determinant of individual managers' remuneration, particularly in large organizations. Hierarchical position has provided the basis for internal pay structures, whilst individual performance and skills have been recognized partly by pay progression within the job, but primarily by promotion through the job hierarchy.

However, by the 1980s the basis of remuneration policy was beginning to shift (Curnow 1986). The notion of a 'going rate' for pay increases was becoming less important, and more emphasis was given to corporate performance and profitability, and to specific recruitment and retention difficulties. At the level of the individual, there was a move away from job size as the sole or primary basis for pay determination, towards individual contribution, skills and competencies.

Such developments may represent a strategic response to the changing demands faced by organizations. One of the best examples of this argument is provided by Kanter (1990). She suggests that the modern 'post-entrepreneurial' organization needs to reduce its

---

Box 6.1 Factors influencing management remuneration

1 *Job 'size'*
   • responsibility,
   • level in the organizational hierarchy,
   • required knowledge, skills or competencies,
   • external contacts,
   • complexity and decision making.
2 *Individual characteristics*
   • age,
   • experience,
   • qualifications and special skills,
   • contribution and performance,
   • potential.
3 *The labour market*
   • relative scarcity,
   • the 'going rate'.
4 *Product market conditions and the employer's cost structure*
   • industry position,
   • market ambitions and strategies,
   • technology.
5 *Remuneration philosophy*

Source: Developed from Curnow 1986.

---

fixed or invariant employee costs, whilst at the same time improving employee performance. Both are necessary if the organization is to prosper in an increasingly competitive world, and yet the two goals appear at first to be contradictory. The key question is: How are employees to be further motivated, whilst at the same time making the pay bill more flexible?

One answer is to base pay on individual and group contribution. 'Post-entrepreneurial' pay systems will therefore consist of relatively low levels of basic guaranteed pay, along with performance bonuses, profit sharing and a range of other incentives designed to win commitment and encourage enterprise at the individual and group level. The consequence is that remuneration packages will become more complex and differentiated as no single factor dominates remuneration policy in the way that job size once did (Kanter 1990; Incomes Data Services 1990b; Mahoney 1992).

However, the challenge facing remuneration planners is not simply to identify and adopt state of the art solutions, but rather to develop a fit between remuneration and HR policies and the strategic aims of the organization, such that the former contribute towards the achievement of the latter. The implication of this is that particular approaches to remuneration will not necessarily be universally applicable.

The aims of remuneration strategy are various, including the recruitment and retention of skilled staff, their effective motivation towards meeting organizational objectives, the management of corporate culture, and even the creation of a favourable public image for the organization. Not surprisingly, such multiple aims may at times conflict and remuneration policy often involves an attempt to balance the tradeoffs between them. Furthermore, remuneration planners have sometimes been less than explicit about what exactly they are trying to achieve, so that the clarification of objectives is an important first step in designing a remuneration policy.

Job evaluation: From job size to competencies

The above developments are to some extent reflected in approaches to job evaluation. Given the traditional focus on job size and on organizational hierarchy, job evaluation has come to play a key role in the determination of managerial pay structures, particularly in larger organizations. A variety of both whole-job and analytical types of system have been used, and management consultants offer many off-the-peg and customized schemes.

With whole-job systems, jobs are compared directly and placed by the evaluators in a hierarchy or grade, according to their perceived value or seniority. These internal relativities between jobs are then used as the basis for the internal pay structure. The drawback of such systems is that they are highly subjective, since those responsible for the evaluation are not encouraged to systematically analyse or justify their job rankings, and traditional assumptions on relative job values are left unchallenged.

Analytical job evaluation schemes involve a more systematic analysis of jobs in terms of underlying 'factors', such as required knowledge, decision making and accountability. Individual jobs are allocated a points score against each of the factors, and a total score is calculated for each job, usually with pre-determined weights attached to the factors in proportion to their relative importance. Points scores may then be used to allocate jobs to salary grades, or alternatively pay may be determined directly from the points score via a numerical formula.

Analytical schemes are preferred to whole-job schemes for equal opportunities reasons. Nevertheless, whilst analytical schemes give the appearance of greater objectivity, all job evaluation ultimately rests not only upon the judgement of those evaluating the jobs, but also on the assumptions underlying the design of the scheme, and in particular the choice and weighting of the factors. Thus, great care is needed in the design of schemes and the definition and weighting of factors must be such that they do not arbitrarily discriminate against women or minority groups.

Aside from problems of subjectivity and bias, job evaluation can also be criticized as a costly and bureaucratic procedure. It is based on given job descriptions and has as its rationale the ordering of jobs into a hierarchy:

> In the '60s and '70s, when many organizations first introduced formal job evaluation processes, the dominant issue was internal equity, and the focus was very much on jobs rather than people. External markets were – or at least were assumed to be – relatively homogeneous, and issues of individual performance and contribution were to a large degree optional extras or accommodated by highly structured systems which often bore more than a passing resemblance to automatic progression. (Murlis and Pritchard 1991: 49)

Job evaluation may no longer be appropriate where the primary concern is with flexibility and performance, where fixed job descriptions are less common, and where organizations are delayering.

However, recent innovations in job evaluation techniques go some way to meeting the criticisms. Computer packages may take away much of the routine administrative burden. Some consultants are redesigning their schemes to make them more sensitive to the competencies and personal qualities demanded by particular jobs, for example by redefining a factor such as 'leadership' to focus on the motivational demands of a job rather than simply recording the number of subordinates supervised (*IDS Top Pay Review*, 133, March 1992: 21).

Many organizations have been reassessing their approach, and a number of them were moving away from traditional job evaluation by the early 1990s. However, whilst job size is becoming less important than in previous decades, there is still likely to be a need for an equitable system of internal relativities, so that some form of job evaluation is likely to be around for some time.

Paying for performance

Merit pay has long been a feature of many organizations. However, traditionally it was largely restricted to managers in the private sector, whilst the public sector and industries such as banking and finance were dominated by incremental salary scales. During the high inflation of the 1970s and early 1980s, merit rewards were largely overshadowed by large cost of living pay increases.

Since the early 1980s, organizations have increasingly been seeking to 'incentivize' remuneration, particularly for managers, in an attempt to improve both individual and organizational performance. This has taken several forms, including not only performance-related pay, but also performance-related cash bonuses and executive share option schemes. In this section, we provide an overview of practice in each of these three areas, concluding with a discussion of the coordination of incentives.

Performance-related pay (PRP)

Performance-related pay is usually based on a systematic salary structure, a formal appraisal system, and a more or less systematic link between appraised performance and individual rewards.

According to a UK survey of 360 organizations carried out in 1991, 66 per cent of private-sector and 34 per cent of public-sector organizations provided PRP for their managers and professional staff, with 58 per cent and 28 per cent respectively providing it for their directors and senior executives. The coverage of PRP schemes had increased markedly since the early 1980s, and whilst it was still used more for managers and professionals than for other staff, it was increasingly being extended to cover more junior employees (Cannell and Wood 1992: 44–6).

In the UK, PRP was used more widely in the private sector than in the public sector, though its use was increasing in the latter – for example, in local government, the civil service and the National Health Service. Indeed, the Conservative government was strongly committed to the extension of PRP, seeing it as having a key role to play in improving the quality of service offered to users of public services.

On the basis of interviews with personnel managers from 44 organizations, Cannell and Wood (1992: 50–65) identify six key reasons why organizations were adopting PRP:

1   due to problems with incremental pay scales, including inflexibility and an inability to reward individual contribution;
2   to reward and motivate staff;
3   to promote cultural and organizational change;
4   to improve communication on performance standards;
5   to improve recruitment and retention, particularly in the public sector;
6   to individualize employee relations.

There are several issues to be considered in designing a PRP scheme. Firstly, what criteria are to be used to assess performance? Whilst traditional merit-pay schemes tended to involve appraisal on the basis of personality traits, more recently there has been a trend towards appraising managers in terms of actual job performance, usually in the form of measurable working objectives (Fowler 1988). This allows individual objectives to link into corporate objectives as part of corporate performance management (see, for example, Mumford and Buley 1988).

However, care must be exercised, since inappropriate performance objectives may produce perverse results. For example, to target branch or sales managers solely on current sales may lead them to place less emphasis on long-term customer relationships, thus possibly damaging the firm's reputation and customer loyalty. However, the risk of such short-termism may be minimized by a careful choice of performance objectives, perhaps including financial targets evaluated over a period of years, or objectives specifically related to customer care or staff development. Box 6.2 provides an example of a company attempting to influence managerial behaviour in a direction which is consistent with corporate objectives.

A second issue to be considered is the nature of the link between appraisal ratings and pay. Many organizations favour a mechanical link, with performance ratings feeding through directly into specific pay increases (see box 6.3). This has the advantage of simplicity and predictability. Individuals can understand the rationale behind their pay increase, and the system can be seen to be fair.

Budgetary control may be exercised by imposing a forced distribution of appraisal and salary outcomes on departmental and unit

Box 6.2 The greening of PRP

Businesses have been under growing pressure to minimize the environmental damage of their operations, by reducing their output of harmful waste and by making more efficient use of non-renewable resources. Public pressure, along with actual and anticipated legislation, and action from bodies such as the National Rivers Authority has led companies to commit themselves to improvement targets. By the late 1980s ICI, the UK's largest chemicals company, was under pressure to improve its environmental performance.

In November 1990, ICI announced a set of environmental objectives, against which performance could be measured and action plans formulated. The four group-wide objectives were as follows:

1 'All new ICI plants will be built to standards capable of meeting all regulations that might reasonably be expected in the most environmentally demanding country in which ICI will operate that process.'
2 'ICI will reduce waste from its operations by 50 per cent by 1995, paying particular attention to that which is hazardous.'
3 'To establish an even more rigorous programme for conserving energy and resources, paying particular attention to actions to safeguard the environment.'
4 'To set up waste-recycling programmes in-house and also in collaboration with customers.'

Environmental spending was to be doubled to £1 billion worldwide and output of harmful wastes was to be cut by at least 50 per cent over the coming five years.

The environmental targets were to be included in ICI's performance management system, with corporate targets being cascaded down to business unit and operating site level, and thence to individual managers. Here, the environmental targets would form part of senior managers' PRP assessment, along with more traditional objectives. Ultimately, ICI aimed to extend this to all staff.

Sources: ICI *Annual Report* 1990; *The ICI Policy on the Environment*, ICI brochure, July 1991; *Financial Times*, 5 December 1990: 12 and 37; interviews with ICI managers.

managers (see box 6.4). This has the advantage of controlling the costs of salary awards and countering any tendency towards leniency or the clustering of appraisals in the middle categories. The disadvantage, however, is that high performers may lose out if they

---

Box 6.3 Linking pay and appraisals: A mechanical approach

Appraisal rating	*Salary award this year*
Outstanding	Scale adjustment plus 6 per cent
Highly effective	Scale adjustment plus 4 per cent
Effective	Scale adjustment plus 2 per cent
Adequate*	Scale adjustment only
Unacceptable**	Nil

*Includes those not eligible for performance-linked increase, for example because they have been in the job for only a few weeks.
** Staff subject to disciplinary action.

Box 6.4 A forced distribution

Appraisal rating	*Required proportions at departmental or unit level*	
Outstanding	20 per cent maximum	} 60 per cent maximum
Highly effective		
Effective		} 40 per cent minimum
Adequate	5 per cent minimum	

---

happen to be part of a unit with an unusually high proportion of good performers, with possible adverse consequences for morale. For this reason, it is desirable to have at least some flexibility to depart from the recommended distribution in exceptional cases.

Alternatively, a more complex guide chart may be devised, linking pay increases not only to the appraisal rating, but also to the individual's existing position in the salary range. Usually this provides for larger increases for those below the salary mid-point, but more modest increases thereafter.

Some organizations dispense with such mechanical approaches, preferring instead to allow line managers to exercise greater discretion and flexibility in the pay rises awarded. There was some evidence that more organizations were adopting this flexible approach in the 1990s (Thompson 1992: 67). Line managers may be issued with guidelines on the suggested pattern of increases according to performance category, but are given discretion to vary the actual rises awarded within a fixed budget. Line managers are thus given even greater discretion, which may be consistent with a policy of increasing their responsibility for human resources. However, there may be more scope for inconsistency between raters than under a more mechanical system, and this may undermine its acceptability.

A third issue in PRP is who should be responsible for conducting performance appraisals. Whilst there are a number of possibilities (see chapter 3), the usual approach is for the manager's immediate superior to carry out the appraisal, possibly with a check on consistency being carried out at a higher level, or by the personnel department.

A fourth issue concerns the role of the trade union, particularly in the public sector and recently privatized corporations, where middle and even relatively senior managers had hitherto had their terms and conditions determined by collective bargaining. Unions have traditionally viewed PRP with suspicion, seeing it as an attempt to undermine collective bargaining, and expressing concern at its subjectivity and the scope for arbitrary and unfair treatment (Industrial Relations Services 1991e).

Union resistance may be minimized by adopting an open approach. At Manchester Airport, for example, when PRP was introduced for middle managers, the employer attempted to secure commitment from individuals by establishing a joint committee with their trade union to oversee the implementation of the scheme (Incomes Data Services no date: 47). The employer may also provide a right of appeal against an adverse appraisal, and the union may be involved by management in a joint monitoring of the scheme.

The introduction of PRP for managers has sometimes involved their removal from collective bargaining. However, there is no necessary relationship between PRP and derecognition, and the union may continue to negotiate on the basic scale adjustments, on the size of award for the 'standard' performer, or on the total pool of money available for merit increases each year.

Finally on PRP, there has been some controversy over whether pay should be linked to appraisals at all. Those opposed to PRP have argued that the appraisal process is more open, and hence more effective in terms of reviewing performance and developing potential, when there is no link with pay. Against this, it is argued that the pay element is important in encouraging managers, as both appraisers

Box 6.5 Job competencies and pay

Some organizations have incorporated 'competencies' into salary determination, in an attempt to move away from inflexible job descriptions and grade hierarchies, and instead to reward and encourage individual performance and development.

Such systems begin by grouping jobs into tiers or 'families', each with a broad salary range (see the graph for an example). The individual's pay then depends on their performance rating and their competency level. The performance rating is determined in the usual way: as an assessment against annual objectives, perhaps on a five-point scale.

Competencies are defined for a job family, and for managers may cover such areas as decision making, dealing with change, and leadership. Twenty or more separate competencies are identified. Levels of competency are carefully defined for each of these, with clear criteria, so that each individual can be assessed in terms of their overall competency level. For example, five competency levels may be defined, from E the lowest, basic level to A the highest.

Appraisal is concerned with both performance and competencies, looking at annual objectives, and also at the development of the individual in terms of the defined competency levels.

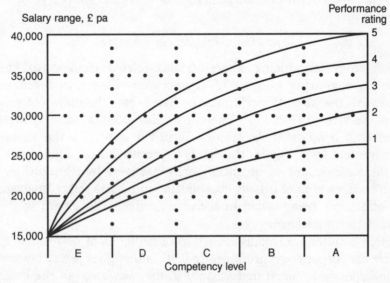

Pay curves for a job tier/family.

For each job family, a set of pay curves in defined, one curve for each performance rating (see the graph). The individual's maximum salary is then given by the point on a salary curve which corresponds to their performance rating and assessed competency level. This can be treated as a flexible maximum, so that individuals may not automatically progress to this level in a given year, allowance being made for market conditions and for the organization's ability to pay. Those who are currently paid in excess of their maximum may be awarded little or no pay increase.

Sources: Armstrong and Murlis, 1991: 541–4; *IDS Top Pay Review*, 137, July 1992: 5–7.

and appraisees, to take the process of objective-setting and appraisal seriously. Furthermore, the incentivization of pay may signal organizational priorities, and form part of an attempt to adjust organizational culture and management style. PRP may be consistent with a move to a more devolved approach, in that line managers are given greater responsibility for determining the pay of their subordinates.

Whilst there were suggestions that some UK managers were becoming disillusioned with PRP in the recession of the early 1990s, innovations continued, and several organizations were linking PRP with the assessment of management competencies (see box 6.5).

Performance-related cash bonuses

Aside from introducing a performance-related element to basic salaries, a growing number of organizations have introduced and increased the size of performance-related cash bonuses (Incomes Data Services 1990b: 9). There has also been a trend towards extending bonuses from senior executives down to the middle-management level. Again, the aim is to incentivize pay and to link it to the achievement of organizational objectives. In addition, since such bonuses are not usually consolidated into basic salary, managers are effectively being asked to accept a greater risk element in their remuneration package.

Such bonuses are usually related to target levels of performance at either the corporate or profit centre level, although it is also common to incorporate personal performance in the calculation of the bonus.

A typical scheme for senior executives would involve an annual lump sum bonus related to the achievement of profit targets. The amount payable on achieving the target might be 30 per cent of basic salary, with the actual amount payable depending on the level of achievement against the target. A threshold level of achievement of, say, 90 per cent of the target might be set as a trigger for bonus payments, with a bonus cap at perhaps 150 per cent of target. In some cases the upper limit may be set rather higher, and some organizations abandoned upper limits altogether in the 1980s.

Some companies set aside a given percentage of pre-tax profit over and above a specified level to form a 'profit pool', from which executive bonuses are paid. Individual's bonuses may then be paid in proportion to base salary, perhaps adjusted in light of performance against personal objectives. Yet another approach is to base the bonus on a weighted combination of personal and corporate targets, perhaps with greater emphasis being given to corporate targets in the case of senior executives.

Bonus schemes have used a variety of performance measures, including not only pre- or post-tax profits, but also earnings per share, return on capital employed and value added, as well as non-financial targets relating to management tasks and resource utilization levels. The last are particularly suitable for managers outside main-stream line and general management functions, though it may be useful to consider a mix of financial and non-financial targets for all managers. Some organizations have linked bonuses to the achievement of quality and service improvements, in an attempt to underpin the development of a quality culture (see box 6.6).

Some organizations have expressed a preference for corporate or unit as opposed to individual targets, on the grounds that individualized incentives may undermine teamwork and fail to motivate the solid team contributor. However, not all organizations share this view, and teamworking may be encouraged by including team or shared objectives in the individual's appraisal, or by making individual incentive payments conditional on meeting unit targets.

In addition to the more systematic schemes described above, some companies make discretionary or *ad hoc* bonus payments, for example on the achievement of an outstanding result. This offers greater flexibility for the employer. Smaller firms in particular may prefer such an approach, whilst some employers use both a formal bonus scheme and *ad hoc* payments.

Box 6.6   Remuneration and the 'quality culture'

As competition becomes more intense and customers more discerning, organizations are increasingly concerned to improve and maintain the quality of their products and the standards of service offered to customers. By the early 1990s, interest in the ideas of the American and Japanese quality gurus was widespread and TQM promised to be one of the key management ideas of the decade.

Some organizations were beginning to make the link between pay and quality, in an attempt to underpin the 'quality culture'. One approach was to pay an annual cash bonus on the basis of the achievement of specified quality or customer service targets. Such schemes tended to be paid on a group basis, and were often applied to all staff, including managers.

Typical quality indicators used include the following:

• Customer satisfaction surveys – a sample of customers may be surveyed on a regular basis, and the bonus linked to measured improvements in customer satisfaction.
• Delivery or service times – the bonus may be linked to the proportion of deliveries made on time, or to improvements in average turnaround times.
• Levels of waste – the bonus may be linked to target levels of waste as a proportion of total production, or to the cost of obsolete stock.

Whilst some quality indicators may be more expensive to collect than the standard financial or production information, organizations have often seen the extra effort as worthwhile as part of their overall approach to quality management.

However, such initiatives are controversial. Many of the quality gurus have suggested that to pay for quality risks undermining the employee's commitment, replacing this with an instrumental, calculative approach. Instead, they argue that quality improvement should be rewarded with recognition, praise and symbolic rewards. This view may, of course, neglect the fact that cash itself may be seen as a form of recognition, and that there may be an expectation of cash rewards.

Sources: Incomes Data Services 1991b; Drummond and Chell 1992.

Share option schemes

A share option scheme involves granting the employee the option to purchase shares in the company at some future date at a specified price, based on the share price ruling at the date the option was granted. Typically, the employee will only be able to exercise the option to buy the shares after, say, three years have elapsed, and the option is withdrawn if in the meantime the employee leaves the company.

The benefit to the recipient comes partly from any discount offered on the original share price, but mainly from any increase in the market price of the shares following the granting of the option. The value of share options to senior executives can be considerable. In a survey of 113 options exercised by UK company directors during the final quarter of 1991, the median profit received was £62,000, representing a gain of 93 per cent on the cost of the option, with a profit of over £2 million accruing to a director of Glaxo (*IDS Top Pay Review*, 133, March 1992: 2–4). Of course, share prices can also fall, and the potential profit from unexercised share options can disappear overnight.

Share options can provide a substantial benefit without adversely affecting company cash flow. They are usually offered to top managers, and giving them an ownership stake in the company provides a long-term incentive, focusing their attention on growth in shareholder value. Share option schemes also have the advantage of discouraging managers from leaving the company. To the extent that the share price increases over time, the recipient is subject to an increasing 'golden handcuff' effect, since to leave the company prior to the option becoming due means that the option is lost. Arguments against the provision of share options include the possibility that shareholders may be concerned at the dilution of equity implied by the extensive granting of share options.

In the UK, by meeting certain Inland Revenue conditions, a share scheme may gain tax advantages. Before 1984, only all-employee schemes were eligible for Inland Revenue approval, so that schemes restricted to executives or managers were denied the tax advantages. However, the 1984 Finance Act allowed employers to establish Inland Revenue approved share option schemes for selected groups of employees: so-called 'discretionary' schemes.

Many employers sought approval for their executive schemes under the 1984 provisions, so that by the early 1990s discretionary schemes accounted for 70 per cent of all share option schemes approved by the Inland Revenue. By this time, the great majority of large UK companies had such a scheme for senior managers. In spite of calls by successive Chancellors of the Exchequer for the provision of share schemes for a wider range of employees, UK employers

---

Box 6.7   All that glitters . . .

Experts in management remuneration have a tendency to talk in gilded terms. Here are a few examples.

The newly appointed manager may be welcomed with a GOLDEN HELLO. The employer, anxious to attract the right person for the job, may offer managers a one-off cash bonus to entice them away from their current job.

Once hired, the valued manager may be locked into the organization with a GOLDEN HANDCUFF. This time the aim is to deter mobility by making it expensive for the manager to leave. Share option schemes, fixed-term contracts with penalties for early leavers, and company pension schemes are common forms of handcuff, although the development of more portable pensions will undermine the last.

The promise of a GOLDEN HANDSHAKE, a large payoff when the individual leaves the organization, either because of redundancy or the expiry of a fixed contract, may also be used to attract talented people.

The GOLDEN PARACHUTE involves giving an employee a long-term contract, and the right to sue for damages should the organization wish to part company early. The senior employee is thus given some financial security, in what may be a highly demanding and results-orientated situation.

Particularly in the USA, the gold-card treatment may be extended beyond the grave. In 1991, an estimated 15 per cent of Fortune 500 companies provided their top executives with a GOLDEN COFFIN; an agreement to continue to pay a salary to the manager's family for several years, should the manager die whilst still in the job (*The Economist*, 21 September 1991: 97).

---

continued to treat share options primarily as a benefit for senior managers.

Incentivization: A coordinated approach

We saw earlier how in poorly designed incentive schemes, managers' performance objectives may encourage them to focus on short-term sales or profitability at the expense of sound long-term developments. Many employers effectively deal with such problems by adopting a coordinated approach to incentivization, providing a range of incentives aimed at different time scales.

Goodswen (1988), for example, explains how the NatWest Bank adopted a remuneration package consisting of PRP increments, annual cash bonuses linked to the achievement of specific job targets, profit sharing, and a share option scheme for executives and senior managers. The aim was to raise managers' awareness of corporate objectives, with cash bonuses and PRP focusing primarily on the current year's performance, whilst the share option scheme would encourage senior management to look to the longer-term improvement of shareholder value. The key point is that incentivization cannot necessarily be reduced to a single measure. What is required is a strategic approach, mindful of both short-term requirements and long-term priorities.

Pay and performance: The missing link?

Much of the discussion of remuneration continues to focus on incentivization and the management of performance. However, the link between remuneration on the one hand and motivation and performance on the other has been taken almost as a matter of faith. In fact, systematic evidence on the incentive effects of PRP, bonuses and share options is very limited (Incomes Data Services no date: 4–5; Thompson 1992: 19–23).

Recent UK studies of PRP show little sign of a significant impact on performance. A survey of 504 private-sector organizations, carried out in 1991, found that those companies with a performance-management system, of which PRP was often a key element, were no more likely than other companies to have high levels of profit growth (Bevan and Thompson 1991: 38–9). A 1990 survey of PRP schemes in 598 organizations found that employers were often sceptical about the effectiveness of such schemes (*IDS Top Pay Review*, 120, February 1991: 7–8). Similarly, a study of the views of personnel managers found them to be uncertain about the motivational impact of PRP, and most argued that such things as the intrinsic qualities of the job, individual recognition and promotion were key motivators. Furthermore, many suggested that PRP could actually be a demotivator for those getting only a small increase (Cannell and Wood 1992). A study of PRP in the Inland Revenue found that whilst staff were generally supportive of the principle of PRP, few said that it had led them to improve their job performance, and there was a concern that PRP might be a demotivator unless staff could be assured of the fairness of the scheme (Marsden and Richardson 1991).

According to studies in the USA, organizations which have PRP are more likely to experience positive employee attitudes in terms of job and pay satisfaction and employee commitment. However, the studies show no consistent effect on subsequent job performance, and there have been few attempts to test the effect on employee absence and turnover (Heneman 1992: 245–60). Similarly, there is little clear evidence that profit sharing schemes have a direct effect on employee effort or organizational performance (Wright 1986).

Furthermore, few organizations attempt to formally evaluate their own incentive schemes, tending not to have clear criteria against which to evaluate them, and relying at best on subjective assessments of their effectiveness (Cannell and Wood 1992: 84–7; Kessler and Purcell 1992; Thompson 1992). This lack of formal evaluation is all the more disturbing since research suggests that organizations which evaluate their pay schemes are more likely to have successful schemes (Wallace 1990).

Many organizations have sought to justify large pay and benefits increases to senior executives as the reward for improved performance, again in the name of incentivization. However, the link between executive pay and corporate performance has often appeared tenuous, and recent years have seen considerable public criticism of top pay increases (see box 6.8). It may be that the pay rises, bonuses and share option benefits for senior managers, and the PRP and enhanced benefits for other managers, often owe more to the need to recruit and retain key skills in the face of keen labour market competition, than to any well thought out attempt at incentivization.

The textbook approach to motivation would question a simple reliance on remuneration. Pay may be seen as a 'hygiene factor', with achievement, responsibility, advancement and the intrinsic qualities of the work itself all having greater motivational impact (Herzberg et al. 1959). Nevertheless, properly designed remuneration policies can recognize and highlight achievement and advancement, whilst innovations such as PRP may signal corporate priorities to managers, and assist in a process of culture change (Cannell and Wood 1992; Incomes Data Services no date; Thompson 1992). Similarly, whilst the evidence for a direct link between profit sharing and productivity is at best inconclusive, profit sharing may contribute towards changing employee attitudes and creating a greater sense of identification with the company (Wright 1986). On this view, the justi-

Box 6.8 Are top managers paid too much?

In the early 1990s, there was growing criticism from shareholders, unions, politicians and the general public at the size of pay increases being paid to top executives. Criticism grew as deteriorating company performance had little initial impact on top pay rises, and senior executives were accused in the media of setting a poor example in a period when pay restraint was seen as critical in restoring international competitiveness.

The British Labour Party sought to make political capital out of the issue, pointing out that many of the companies paying the largest increases to directors had former Conservative cabinet ministers on their boards. Labour called on the Conservative government to use its remaining 40 per cent shareholding in National Power and PowerGen, the two recently privatized electricity companies, to block proposed directors' pay increases at the annual shareholders' meetings.

Similar controversies raged in the USA, where shareholders themselves were becoming increasingly vocal in their opposition to large pay increase for top managers. The United Shareholders' Association, a lobby group working on behalf of individual shareholders, was amongst those attempting to embarrass companies into limiting the pay increases of their senior executives. In early 1992, the Securities and Exchange Commission bowed to the pressure of shareholder and public opinion and made it easier for shareholders to vote on executive remuneration at the annual shareholders' meeting.

In Australia, the annual general meeting of TNT was the scene of angry debates in 1990, with shareholders objecting to a 39 per cent increase in directors' fees, including a rise of A$390,000 for Sir Peter Abeles, the chief executive, bringing his annual salary to more than A$5 million. Both the then prime minister Bob Hawke and the leader of the opposition John Hewson joined in the ensuing debate, calling for pay restraint by top executives as part of the fight against recession. A government inquiry was set up to investigate the issue.

Were such criticisms well-founded? Evidence on the tenuous link between corporate performance and the remuneration of top managers can be found in each of the three countries. In the UK, a survey of top directors' pay increases for 1990–91 concluded:

'Overall, there was no discernible relationship between company performance and remuneration increases'. (*IDS Top Pay Review*, 126, August 1991: 4)

Similarly, in the USA:

> 'Overall, corporate profits of companies listed on the New York Stock Exchange fell seven per cent last year, but their chief executives' pay and other bonuses rose by a similar amount'. (*The Economist*, 21 September 1991: 97)

A survey of Australia's biggest 100 companies in 1990 found that they gave their chief executive officers an average salary increase of 7.4 per cent, in spite of a decline in average market capitalization of 4 per cent.

Of course, it may be that such pay increases can be justified in terms of cost of living increases, the state of the labour market, or international comparisons. In the UK, such rises can also be seen partly as a restoration of pay differentials, following the relative decline of management pay during the 1970s.

The point is, however, that top managers had received pay increases well above the national average during the 1980s, and these had usually been justified to shareholders, employees and the general public as an incentive and as a reward for improved performance. Not surprisingly, this had created an expectation that top managers would share the bad times as well as the good.

Companies took a number of steps to try to head off such criticism. Several British companies changed their accounting procedures to allow them to declare bonuses in the year in which they are earned, rather than in the following year when they are paid out. This may avoid having large bonuses being paid out for last year's good results when performance has meanwhile deteriorated.

Another British innovation, supported by the institutional investors, the Bank of England and the Director General of the Institute of Directors, is to follow the example of most large US corporations in establishing a remuneration committee consisting mainly of non-executive directors. This suggestion has also found support in Australia. The argument is that such a committee can determine executive remuneration free from suspicions of self-interest, and so demonstrate that the interests of the business and shareholders are being respected.

However, in practice such committees do not appear to have restrained executive pay in either the UK or the USA, suggesting that the formation of a remuneration committee may be insufficient to offset public and shareholder criticisms (Main and Johnston 1992). Top executives are, after all, a highly visible group of employees, and with issues of corporate governance and social responsibility now firmly on the agenda, the debate on executive pay is likely to run and run.

fication for many of the so-called 'incentivizing' innovations need not necessarily rest on any direct link from cash to effort, and may have more to do with changing attitudes and culture.

Furthermore, the proponents of incentive pay would argue that just because the balance of evidence does not point to a clear link between incentives and performance, this does not necessarily mean that such a link cannot be achieved. The research evidence may simply reflect poorly designed or badly implemented attempts at incentivization. We return to this point in the conclusions to the chapter, where we draw together our arguments and offer some guidance on the use of incentives.

Benefits

The managerial remuneration package may consist of a range of cash and non-cash benefits, including basic salary, bonus, pension, car, share options and other fringe benefits. There are several reasons for offering a package of benefits, rather than simply providing the whole amount in cash. Firstly, the employee typically has a diversity of needs and expectations, including current income, longer-term security, recognition and status. Cash may not necessarily be the most effective way of satisfying each of these. Status may be more effectively demonstrated through a conspicuous benefit such as a company car, whilst an occupational pension scheme may be the best way of providing longer-term security. Careful remuneration planning may thus maximize the subjective valuation placed on the package by the employee, and more effectively meet the organization's objectives.

Secondly, innovation in the provision of employee benefits may be driven by competition for managerial talent. This explains the bandwagon effect which often appears as organizations struggle to provide a package which matches that of rivals in the recruitment market. This was particularly marked in the case of public-sector organizations in the UK during the late 1980s, when there was a scramble to develop managerial packages which could compete more effectively with the private sector.

Thirdly, certain employee benefits may have the status of what economists call 'merit goods'. For example, an employer may provide private health insurance to try to ensure that staff absence due to sickness is minimized, and that treatment is available at a time which fits in with the employer's needs. Fourthly, remuneration planners are often concerned to provide a package which minimizes the tax liability for both employer and employee, so that remuneration policies may be highly sensitive to fiscal changes.

Whilst much of the discussion of benefits centres on the relative costs and tax implications, it is important to recognize the impact of broader social trends on this aspect of remuneration policy. For example, the growing number of women managers and dual-income families means that organizations may consider childcare assistance as an important benefit in the future (see chapter 7). Similarly, the suggestion that managers generally have become less willing to move house, or even to travel as part of the job, means that benefits policies may have to adapt – for example, by providing greater assistance with staff relocation, perhaps to the extent of helping spouses to find work in the new area.

In this section, we focus on some of the more widespread benefits and attempt to give a flavour of the main trends in benefits policies.

Pensions

Pensions have become a key element in managerial remuneration. They represent deferred pay and are critical in providing employees with long-term security. Whilst for younger staff the pension may appear remote and be of little immediate interest, for more senior employees pension may be the key benefit when it comes to considering a job move.

In the UK, company or occupational pension schemes usually involve contributions from both the employer and the employee, though non-contributory schemes, where only the employer contributes, are common for managerial staff. Schemes can be submitted to the Inland Revenue for approval. The Inland Revenue places limits on the level of benefits payable, with a maximum pension of two-thirds of the individual's final salary under approved schemes. Approval brings important tax advantages, not least of which is that contributions attract full tax relief. The great majority of schemes are of the approved type.

The most common form of occupational pension scheme for those working in large UK companies has been the 'final salary' scheme. Such schemes provide a pension related to length of service and the individual's salary at or near retirement. For example, a scheme may entitle the employee to 1/60th of final salary for each year of service, so that someone retiring after 35 years' service would receive a pension of 35/60ths of their final salary. 'Final salary' is as defined by the particular scheme. For example, it may be taken as the salary earned in the year prior to retirement, or as the average of the best three years' salary during the last ten. Contributions are determined by actuarial calculation, given the need to have sufficient funds to meet anticipated benefits.

Final salary schemes have the advantage to the employee of providing a predictable level of benefits, related to salary on retirement. However, this brings disadvantages to the employer, in that contributions must be sufficient to provide the specified level of benefits and so are not necessarily predictable over the long term. Particularly in times of high inflation, when pension entitlements increase very rapidly due to rising salaries, it may be necessary to increase contributions to counter underfunding of schemes.

An alternative approach is the 'money purchase' scheme. Pension contributions made by and on behalf of an individual are used to provide pension benefits for that particular individual. Each employee has an identifiable fund accumulated on their behalf. The cost to the employer is more predictable than with final salary schemes, since contributions can be set at a given sum or percentage of salary. However, while employees may be attracted to the idea of having an annual statement of their own fund, the level of benefits is less certain than under a final salary scheme.

Money purchase schemes have often been used for senior executives who, under a so-called 'top hat' scheme, may be provided with an individualized pension, with a higher level of contributions and benefits than for other employees. This has been a popular way of providing additional pension benefits for senior managers, since any such provisions made under a general final salary scheme have had to be reported to the whole membership of the scheme.

Pensions have been the most common 'golden handcuff', since those leaving a company pension scheme early have traditionally been heavily penalized by poor transfer values when seeking to enter an alternative scheme. However, there has been growing concern that this restricts job mobility, and recent governments have been keen to increase the flexibility of pension arrangements and to provide for greater individual choice. Recent UK legislation has improved the position of early leavers under final salary schemes, and employees now have the right to opt for a personal pension. The latter allows the individual to purchase a fully-portable personal pension plan from a financial institution, rather than remain in membership of the state earnings-related pension scheme or an occupational scheme. The legislation also allows for the employer to make contributions towards such a personal pension.

The legislation on personal pensions initially attracted concern from remuneration planners, since membership of the company pension scheme could no longer be a condition of employment. The fear was that company schemes would be undermined, particularly as younger employees might find personal pensions more attractive. In the event, by the early 1990s most employers still favoured the provision of an occupational scheme, even for their senior managers, and most did not encourage employees to opt for personal pensions. However, the introduction of personal pensions did appear to have some impact, with employers attempting to make their schemes more attractive, for example by improving benefits, introducing new contributions rates, and improving the benefits on early retirement (*IDS Top Pay Review*, 115, September 1990: 7).

The British government's 1989 budget saw the introduction of an upper earnings limit for the calculation of pension under tax-approved final salary schemes, effectively placing a ceiling on benefits for all new entrants to such schemes. This 'earnings cap' was initially set at £60,000, and would be increased annually in line with prices. Employers seeking to provide pension benefits over and above this level would have to establish top-up schemes, which would not attract tax relief. Alternatively, they might provide additional salary to compensate affected employees. One possible effect will be to encourage employers to offer greater flexibility and choice between pension and other benefits (see below).

The general trend in pensions is towards greater portability, so that the traditional 'handcuff' effect is likely to diminish. It remains to be seen whether there will be a widespread shift to personal pensions. Come what may, it seems likely that pensions will remain a key area of remuneration management in the 1990s, not least because the ageing labour force means that a greater number of managers will be expressing a keen interest in the value of their pension benefits.

Company cars

Whilst the pension is the most widespread benefit, the company car is surely the most discussed. Its major significance is as a highly visible status symbol, and those in receipt of a company car typically drive a rather larger model than they would otherwise provide for themselves. In addition to the value of the use of the car, there is the benefit of the relief from the worries of car purchase, depreciation and maintenance. Add to this the fact that, at least until the late 1980s, it was a highly tax-efficient form of remuneration in the UK, and it is hardly surprising that the company car became a key benefit for managers. During the 1980s, the number of company cars in Britain increased fourfold, with around two million people benefiting by 1992. In 1989, company cars accounted for 60 per cent of all new car sales in Britain (*Observer*, 7 January 1990: 8).

It is normal practice for UK employers to provide cars on both a user basis, to those with a minimum business mileage, and to more senior staff on the basis of status. The great majority of UK senior and middle managers qualify for a car on at least one of these criteria. Tax, insurance and maintenance are usually paid for by the employer, although free fuel for private use is usual only for more senior managers. Those few unfortunate British managers not in receipt of a car are likely to receive either a mileage allowance to cover the cost of petrol and depreciation when their own vehicle is used for business purposes, or possibly a cash allowance as a contribution towards providing their own car.

There has been some public concern at the level of company car provision in Britain, which is far higher than in the USA, Japan and other European countries, particularly at middle-management level. The widespread provision of company cars is said to contribute to road congestion and pollution, and to distort transport choices by effectively subsidizing motoring relative to public transport.

After 1979, successive Chancellors of the Exchequer sought to eliminate the tax distortions which had contributed to the proliferation of fringe benefits. Lower rates of income tax and the heavier taxation of company cars shifted the balance of tax efficiency. By the late 1980s, many commentators were suggesting that saturation point in the provision of company cars must soon be reached. However, the provision of company cars continued to increase, particularly in local government and the financial services sector. Thus, at least initially, heavier taxation appeared to have little impact on the provision of company cars.

It may be that the non-tax advantages are sufficient to sustain the company car. However, the introduction of employers' national insurance contributions on cars led some employers to reconsider, and by 1992 many were considering offering staff a cash alternative (*The Director*, April 1992: 75–8). The British government's proposal to tax cars on the basis of list price from 1994 was expected to lead to significant tax increases for the models usually offered to middle and senior managers, and to give a further push in this direction (Incomes Data Services 1992).

Health insurance

Private health insurance became increasingly popular in Britain during the 1980s. By 1992 an estimated 12 per cent of Britons were covered (*Financial Times*, 11 May 1992: 12). At senior management level in particular, health insurance had become a standard part of the remuneration package, with over 80 per cent of directors receiving free medical insurance by 1989 (*IDS Top Pay Review*, 104, October 1989: 2–4). In many cases, cover was extended to the employee's family.

Private health insurance may be provided free. Alternatively, the employee may be required to pay either part or the whole premium. However, a major benefit to the employee is that corporate schemes usually attract a discount on what would be available to the individual.

Health insurance provides a degree of security for the employee, with the advantage to the employer of ensuring that key staff receive prompt, high quality treatment, thus contributing to effective performance. It can also be seen as a status benefit, provided free only to those above a given job level, and particularly in the public sector it has often been seen as enabling the organization to compete for senior staff.

By the early 1990s, UK employers were becoming concerned about the rising cost of private health insurance, as premiums were increasing faster than the general price level. Various measures were being implemented to control costs, including improved administration and tighter controls, the introduction of an excess payment on claims, the vetting of all claims by senior management, encouraging employees to make more use of NHS facilities, and the exclusion of retired employees from cover. Some employers were reconsidering health insurance and exploring alternative ways of providing health care for their employees, such as by-passing insurance schemes completely and setting up company healthcare trusts (*IDS Top Pay Review*, 115, September 1990: 4–6).

Flexibility and choice

Fringe benefits can account for anything up to 50 per cent of a manager's remuneration. Given the competition for managerial talent and the rising cost of many benefits, it is vital that organizations manage their benefits package effectively. One innovation which seeks to maximize the value of remuneration in terms of employee satisfaction is the so-called 'cafeteria' system.

Under a cafeteria benefits system, employees are provided with a range of 'core' benefits, usually including a basic salary level and pension entitlement, and are then able to choose the remaining elements of their remuneration package from amongst a range of options. Particular schemes vary in terms of the degree of flexibility and range of benefits offered, but may involve alternative company cars, various pension, health insurance and life assurance options, additional cash or holidays, and perhaps a choice of less common benefits such as childcare assistance, school fees, and travel season ticket loans. The various choice options have price tags attached to them, and the employee may choose a package up to a given total value.

Given the potentially far-reaching implications of their choices, it is important that staff are provided with full information and counselling on the options available. The benefits of greater flexibility can be easily overshadowed if staff become disillusioned by the lack of guidance.

Cafeteria benefits schemes became popular in the USA during the 1980s, with an estimated growth in the number of schemes from around 50 in 1983 to 800 by 1988 (*IDS Top Pay Review*, 101, January 1989: 2–5; Barber et al. 1992). They are also being more widely used in Australia. In the UK, however, whilst top managers may have a say in the composition of their remuneration package, employers have been slower to introduce flexibility for other managers and staff, due partly to the alleged administrative complexity and taxation pitfalls involved, and also perhaps because of ignorance and inertia on the part of remuneration planners (Woodley 1990).

However, there were signs by the early 1990s that some UK employers were beginning to move towards greater flexibility, with choice on pensions, health insurance and holidays, particularly for senior managers, and also with the possibility of cash or car options. The introduction of the pensions cap and the heavier taxation of company cars may have been influential here. The Mortgage

---

Box 6.9 'Options': Cafeteria benefits at the Mortgage Corporation

'Options' was launched in June 1990, and offered a flexible menu of benefits for 400 managers and staff. A core package was provided as follows:

- basic salary;
- cash bonus;
- holiday entitlement;
- a money purchase pension scheme;
- medical insurance at provincial rates;
- long-term disability pay;
- life assurance;
- a mortage subsidy (for employees with at least one year's service).

Staff were each allocated a monthly Options value, which they could use to buy additional elements. Initially, the choice was limited to increased pension contributions, enhanced medical cover at London rates or to cover the additional family members, or cash, with the possibility of taking some combination of all three. The aim was to widen the range of benefits choice in the future.

The individual's Options value was linked to salary level. For example, in 1990 someone on a basic salary of £20,000 was allocated a monthly Options value of £103, whilst someone on £40,000 got a value of £239 per month. Staff were expected to make their choices on an annual basis, with their package then remaining unchanged for the full year.

Source: *IDS Top Pay Review*, 116, October 1990: 8–9.

Corporation was one of the earliest UK employers to offer a full cafeteria system to all categories of staff, with the launch of its 'Options' package in June 1990 (see box 6.9). Other employers adopting cafeteria systems for managers include BHS in 1991, and Burton Group and the Royal Mail in 1992.

There are several reasons why employers might be advised to consider cafeteria benefits (Woodley 1990). The fall in the birth rate in the 1960s, and the need for employers to seek alternatives to young people, will lead to an increasingly diverse workforce. More women, older workers, part-timers, job sharers and so on will mean that a fixed benefits package will be less likely than ever to meet the needs of everyone, placing flexibility and choice at a premium.

Furthermore, the growing number of dual-income families increases the likelihood of duplication of certain benefits, such as private health insurance, so that employees may value greater flexibility.

Cafeteria benefits may offer employers greater value for money. So far there has been no systematic study of the effects of flexible benefits in the UK, but research in the USA suggests that such schemes increase employee awareness of the value of their benefits package and improve job satisfaction (Barber et al. 1992). Thus, cafeteria systems may help maximize the motivational impact for a given cash outlay.

Recent developments have made it easier to introduce cafeteria benefits. The introduction of computer-aided administration systems makes the complexity of cafeteria schemes less of a problem, and the shift to a more tax-neutral treatment of benefits and cash simplifies the tax implications.

Thus, whilst UK employers were rather slower than their US counterparts to offer cafeteria benefits systems, many commentators were predicting that more flexible packages would be a key development in the UK during the 1990s. Given thorough preparation and research, careful administration, and sensitive communications and counselling, more flexible benefits packages may have much to offer UK organizations and their managers.

Personal contracts: The 'quiet revolution'?

Particularly for senior managers in the private sector, remuneration and conditions have traditionally been determined on an individual basis. In the public sector, and for many middle and junior managers in the private sector, the norm has been for terms and conditions to be determined more or less collectively. In the UK, this has sometimes involved collective bargaining (Bamber 1986).

However, by the end of the 1980s 'personal contracts' were being introduced for senior management in the National Health Service, the Royal Mail, local authorities, and the newly privatized corporations such as British Telecom and the electricity supply industry. A few organizations, notably in newspaper publishing, had begun to offer them to their middle managers and even to more junior staff (Pickard 1990).

Such contracts involve the settling of terms and conditions on an individual basis, and are often for a fixed term. The move to a more flexible and individualized remuneration package, and the appraisal of performance, are taken further with personal contracts, and their introduction has often been accompanied by PRP and bonuses.

In the public sector, personal contracts represent further evidence of a shift towards a private-sector management culture. Some commentators see them as a sign of the individualization of employment relations, and as part of a move away from collective bargaining. There is evidence that the trade unions are concerned about the impact on their members and on the union's role, and the introduction of such contracts has sometimes been associated with union derecognition (Pickard 1990). Others are sceptical about the long-term significance of personal contracts, seeing them simply as a reflection of the industrial relations and personnel management climate of the late 1980s, which will pass as circumstances change. Whichever view proves correct, it is difficult to envisage a move back to national collective bargaining for the majority of managers in the public utilities.

Summary and conclusions

Whilst organizations have made significant changes in their remuneration policies, some have seen the response of employers as largely piecemeal and conservative. Innovations have often been driven by short-term recruitment and retention difficulties rather than by long-term strategic thinking.

Performance-related payments tend to be a relatively small part of total remuneration, and few organizations have reached Tom Peters' (1989: 332) target of variable incentivized pay equal to at least 25 per cent of base pay for middle and junior managers (Cannell and Wood 1992: 70–1). Furthermore, the once and for ever nature of many PRP rises appears to reflect a continuing belief in the legitimacy of upward pay progression, as opposed to the 'here and now' reward of contribution, and still emphasizes the importance of hierarchical relationships through the appraisal process (Kanter 1990: 233).

However, we must not be over-critical. Such views are based on ideal notions of what remuneration policies should be like, and perhaps pay insufficient attention to the organizational context, and to the difficulties of implementing radical change in the short term. Managerial remuneration is becoming increasingly complex and differentiated, as organizations seek to involve managers in the pursuit of quality, flexibility and performance. Whilst there is no simple link between pay and performance, the remuneration packages of the 1990s are seeking to reward individual and group contribution. In the flatter and less hierarchical organizations of the future, remuneration policy looks set to perform many of the recognition and reward functions previously performed by promotion. Incentivization will remain an important theme, and remuneration policies will play a key role in changing employee attitudes and corporate culture.

Given the likely key role of incentives, it is worth re-emphasizing some basic rules. Bearing in mind our earlier discussion of their possible limitations, if incentives are to have a significant impact on attitudes or behaviour they should be:

- related to objectives over which the individual can have significant influence;
- visible to all concerned;
- transparent, in the sense that the method of calculation and the relationship between contribution and rewards should be made clear;
- significant in relation to total remuneration – hence the view of many experts that effective incentivization requires a shrinking of the share of guaranteed pay: 10 to 15 per cent of base pay is an often-quoted minimum level for an effective incentive, though, as we have seen, Tom Peters has argued for 25 per cent; furthermore, incentive payments should not be restricted to a tiny minority of 'star' performers, if the majority are to see a link between their own pay and performance;
- prompt – whilst time scales for the measurement of contribution and the distribution of reward may be longer for managers than for more junior employees, rewards need to follow performance without undue delay, and many organizations have used prompt one-off rewards to good effect.

Most importantly, an effective remuneration policy amounts to more than simply throwing money at staff. The key aim is to maintain commitment by involving managers in the success of the organization. Remuneration policy can be only one element in this, and there must be consistency with other HRM policies. For example, where incentives are offered, managers must feel that they are capable of meeting the goals and so contributing to organizational performance. Skills gaps and organizational barriers must be confronted. Effective incentivization thus has implications for training and development policies, and for the way in which the organization is managed.

Flexibility and the individualization of remuneration will also be key themes in the future. Whether this will take the form of cafeteria benefits remains to be seen, but organizations will need to be sensitive to the needs of an increasingly diverse and demanding managerial workforce, and must compete effectively in the managerial labour market. The move towards greater tax neutrality between cash and other benefits offers an opportunity for a more strategic approach.

Finally, those responsible for the management of remuneration must be aware of the demands of their own organization and its environment. Whilst there are common themes in remuneration policy, the challenge facing organizations is not so much the search for a panacea, as the development of a remuneration strategy which meets the needs of the particular organization and which is consistent with its overall approach to the management of managers.

Further reading

A comprehensive UK treatment of remuneration practice is provided by Michael Armstrong and Helen Murlis, *Reward Management: A Handbook of Remuneration Strategy and Practice*, second edition, London: Kogan Page, 1991. For useful studies of the impact of incentive pay see Marc Thompson, *Pay and Performance: The Employer Experience*, IMS Report 218, Brighton: Institute of Manpower Studies, 1992; and Michael Cannell and Stephen Wood, *Incentive Pay: Impact and Evolution*, London: IPM, 1992.

7

Women in Management

Women in Britain, as in other countries, continue to miss out on employment and promotion opportunities. This is in spite of the Sex Discrimination Act of 1975, which outlawed discrimination in employment. The lack of equal opportunities is particularly evident in managerial occupations, with talk of a 'glass ceiling' through which women find it difficult to rise. Concern has mounted in recent years, with employers, unions, women's groups and politicians increasingly making statements on the need to recruit and retain greater numbers of women in managerial and professional occupations.

This concern arises for at least three reasons. Firstly, for reasons of equity.｜Where particular women have qualifications, experience and skills that are equal or superior to their male colleagues, to deny them access to more senior jobs is simply unfair. Given that greater numbers of women are now entering further and higher education, it is not surprising that the demand for equal opportunities has grown.｜ Secondly, an image as an equal opportunities employer may be useful to the organization in public relations terms. Women are, after all, customers, and in many industries they account for a majority of purchases.

Thirdly, women represent an underutilized resource for employers. Demographic trends point to a marked decline in the number of young people in the labour market, and many employers are looking for alternative sources of labour (Lennon 1990). Also, in an increasingly competitive economy, human resources may play a key role in determining competitive advantage, so that employers who choose not to train and develop their women employees are not making the best use of their workforce. Again, equal opportunities are in the best interests of employers.

The above arguments apply not only to women, but also to other groups which have often been underutilized by employers. Ethnic minorities, older workers and people with disabilities have found it particularly difficult to progress into managerial and professional occupations. Whilst we focus on women, much of what we say also applies to these other groups, particularly our discussion of the ways in which employers may promote equal opportunities.

We begin the chapter by showing that women are under-represented in management, especially at more senior levels. We examine various explanations for this, and we review the experience of women who have broken through the 'glass ceiling' into management. We then discuss what employers can do to promote equal opportunities, and we consider the likely impact of such policies on the prospects for women managers in the future. We conclude with some summary points of guidance for management on the promotion of equal opportunities.

Women in management: Some evidence.

Although women made up around 43 per cent of the total work-force, in 1990 only 28 per cent of British managers were women (OPCS various years). The proportion of women managers falls sharply at the more senior levels, and it is estimated that fewer than 5 per cent of UK company directors are women (Policy Studies Institute 1991). In general, there are relatively few women at the top of the occupational hierarchy (see box 7.1).

Where women do break through into managerial jobs, they tend to be concentrated in particular functions, such as personnel and training, administration and public relations (Coe 1992: 7). Women managers tend to work in specialist support roles, and are less likely than men to be found in line and general management (Nicholson and West 1988; Hirsh and Jackson 1990). Women managers also tend to be in sectors which employ large numbers of women. Almost a quarter of all women managers work in retail distribution (Equal Opportunities Commission 1991: 15–16), and in 1992 most female managing directors and chief executives worked for companies involved in fashion, toiletries, restaurants or children's goods (*Financial Times*, 20 January 1992: 6).

Studies have shown that women managers tend to be younger than their male colleagues, they tend to have been with their current employer for a shorter period of time, they are more likely to be single

Box 7.1 Women at the top in the UK

Job	Number of women	Total jobs
Cabinet ministers	0	22
Government ministers	7	108
Civil service		
Permanent secretaries (grade 1)	0	35
Deputy permanent secretaries	11	131
ICI directors	1 (non-exec)	17
Marks and Spencer directors	1 (non-exec)	20
BP directors	0	17
Barclays Bank directors	1 (non-exec)	23
Lloyds Bank directors	0	23
Midland Bank directors	1 (non-exec)	16
NatWest Bank directors	1 (non-exec)	22
Judges		
Lords of Appeal	0	10
Appeal Court judges	1	27
High Court judges	2	82
Circuit judges	20	439
Local council chief executives	6	450
Trade union general secretaries	2	74
National newspaper editors	2	21
Secondary school head teachers	1,000 approx	4,000
British Coal directors	0	12
British Rail directors	2 (non-exec)	13
Post Office directors	0	11
Police Force		
Chief constables	0	43
Assistant chief constables	3	127
Chief superintendents	11	551
National Health Service managers	3,500 approx	10,000

Source: *Financial Times*, 29 October 1991: 10.

and childless, and have better formal qualifications (see, for example, Davidson and Cooper 1983: 96; Alban-Metcalfe and Nicholson 1984: 41; Nicholson and West 1988: 186–91; Scase and Goffee 1989: 106; NEDO/RIPA 1990: 33; Coe 1992: 9). The findings on marital status and children are particularly significant, and are likely to reflect the unequal distribution of domestic responsibilities, with marriage and family responsibilities being much more of a career disadvantage for women than for men (Nicholson and West 1988: 188–9; NEDO/RIPA 1990: 34; Coe 1992: 11).

Why are there so few women managers?

The small numbers of women managers can be explained partly in terms of education and occupational choice, and partly by what happens to women once they enter the labour market. The latter may involve several factors, including discrimination in recruitment and barriers to promotion for women already in employment. We consider these issues in turn.

Education and occupational choice

The predominance of men in managerial and professional occupations is to some extent a reflection of the fact that they have tended to be more highly qualified than women. However, this difference is greater for older age groups, and the gap is closing. In particular, women have been taking a growing share of places in higher education in the UK, accounting for 35 per cent of all higher education qualifications obtained in 1981 and 42 per cent by 1988 (*Social Trends*, 22, 1992: 63).

However, whilst such trends bode well for the future access of women to higher-level job opportunities, there is still evidence of sex-stereotyping in educational choices. Girls are still more likely to achieve GCSE grade C or better in English, History, Biology and French, whilst boys are more likely to do so in Maths, Physics, Geography and Chemistry (*Regional Trends*, 26, 1991: 141). These differences are reflected in higher and further education, with women being more likely to choose business and social studies, education, nursing, languages and creative arts subjects, whilst men are more likely to opt for engineering, technology and the physical and mathematical sciences (*Education Statistics for the United Kingdom*, 1991: 31).

We would not necessarily expect to see girls and boys making identical subject choices at school and in higher education, but the danger is that even though women's educational achievements have improved relative to those of men, they will continue to be channelled into particular occupations and industries, risking a perpetuation of the stereotypes which have limited women's opportunities in the past. Such stereotypes do seem to have heavily influenced occupational choices. Women tend to opt for traditionally female occupations, and women's own views on occupational stereotypes are often supported by parents and professional advisers (Wilson 1991).

The implication of such stereotyping in occupational choice is that women are crowded into a relatively narrow range of industries and occupations, and this may limit their opportunities for promotion into management. As we have seen, women tend to be sidelined into support functions. The problem here is that it is often more difficult to secure promotion into more senior general management posts from such functions, since experience in the core production function is often seen as an essential prerequisite for promotion into general management positions (Hirsh and Jackson 1990: 24–5). Just as women may face a 'glass ceiling' in securing promotion, so they may also face a 'glass wall' in moving beyond such support functions.

Discrimination in recruitment

However, the crowding of women into particular occupations and industries may not be wholly attributable to their own occupational choices; employer's recruitment practices also have a role to play.

Employer's selection decisions are often made on the basis of informal and highly subjective assessments of both job requirements and of the ability of particular individuals to meet those requirements (see, for example, Curran 1988; Collinson et al. 1990). Rather than adhere to the formalized recruitment and selection model recommended in the textbooks, managers often prefer to rely on their own 'gut feeling' of what the ideal candidate would look like. Indeed, for many managers it is a matter of personal pride that they are a good judge of character and able to pick 'winners'.

One implication of this is that there is scope for selection decisions to be strongly influenced by stereotypical views of jobs and candidates, and indeed by personal prejudices on the part of the selector. Studies have shown that managers often categorize certain jobs as 'male' and others as 'female', so that discrimination at the recruitment stage, whether conscious or not on the part of those responsible, may channel women into particular jobs (Curran 1988; Collinson et al. 1990).

Such a process may be particularly marked in the case of career-related and managerial jobs. Management has often been seen as requiring certain 'male' characteristics, such as decisiveness, assertiveness and drive. According to Rothwell (1985), the stereotypical woman is said to lack such qualities, having been socialized into 'female' attitudes and behaviour, which discourage themselves and others from seeing them as potential managers. However, the criteria involved in the selection of managers are essentially subjective, and Hirsh and Bevan (1988) argue that employers have tended to emphasize the 'male' aspects of the job in a fairly arbitrary manner, so that to exclude women from management positions may owe more to tradition and prejudice than to any rational analysis of job requirements. Furthermore, management selection decisions are often informed by notions of peer-group acceptability, which again has the potential to disadvantage women where the majority of managers are male.

The formalization of the recruitment and selection process is one way to reduce such discrimination. This involves recruiting from as wide a range of sources as possible, rather than relying mainly on informal word of mouth recruitment channels, which tend to produce candidates who mirror the existing workforce. Selection should be based on a rigorous analysis of job requirements and a systematic assessment of candidates against those requirements. Care must be taken to ensure that person specifications do not indirectly discriminate by making unnecessary demands on candidates, and any selection tests must be carefully validated to ensure that they predict job performance and do not discriminate against women.

Promotion and careers

In most occupations and industries, women tend to occupy the more junior positions in the job hierarchy, even in sectors where they account for a majority of employees (Equal Opportunities Commission 1991: 15; Ashburner 1991; Colgan and Tomlinson 1991). Although the number of women recruited into the graduate training schemes of major employers has increased in recent years, this has tended not to lead to an equivalent increase in the numbers of women being promoted into middle management (Hirsh and Jackson 1990: 27).

This suggests that the scarcity of women managers is not simply due to differences between the sexes in education and occupational choices, nor even to discrimination at the initial recruitment stage. In this section, we examine some of the more common arguments put forward to account for the fact that women perform less well than men in terms of promotion and career development.

Firstly, it is often argued that women are less ambitious than men, so that their lack of career progression is to some extent a matter of personal choice. Most employers can provide anecdotal evidence in support of this view. However, surveys of managers often report that women managers are equally or more ambitious than are male managers (Scase and Goffee 1989; Hirsh and Jackson 1990), so that we cannot take it for granted that all women are necessarily less interested in their careers.

A second reason why women find it difficult to move into management is that many organizations have based their employment policies on the assumption of a traditionally 'male' career pattern (see box 7.2). This typically involves an uninterrupted career path, with what appears as a planned sequence of upward job moves, either within or across organizations. To the extent that managers are expected to conform to such a pattern, women are placed at a disadvantage. There are several reasons for this.

Childcare and domestic responsibilities may result in a lack of continuity in employment, so that employers may be reluctant to invest in the career development of women. Women returning to

---

Box 7.2 Some key assumptions about the managerial career

The successful career demands:

- good job performance, reflected in appraisals and informal assessments by superiors;
- continuous employment throughout the career, with a critical career-building phase during the late twenties and thirties;
- that the individual's career phase is strongly related to age;
- the ability and willingness to assume a heavy workload, with long and flexible working hours, as a means of demonstrating commitment to the organization and to a career;
- geographical mobility as part of the career-building process;
- the accumulation of experience in several functions, including the core production activities of the organization, as a prerequisite for advancement into senior management.

work after having had children tend to enter unskilled, low-paid jobs, often on a part-time basis (Dex 1984; Coe 1992). When married women remain at work, they are often less able than men to work the long and flexible hours which have often been expected of managers. Such considerations may occur to employers even before the woman has children, and thus may damage career progress from very early in the career.

A common explanation for the lack of women's career progression in the finance sector and elsewhere is that they are often seen as being less geographically mobile than men. Some employers have valued mobility, particularly in industries with extensive branch networks, and careers have often been based around a series of branch moves. This may discourage women in particular from applying for promotion. However, the mobility issue may simply be a convenient excuse for organizations with few women managers. Resistance to mobility may depend just as much on factors such as the age of children as on sex, and as the number of dual career couples increases, men may also be more reluctant to move.

A third explanation for the small number of women managers is that women may face discrimination in promotion. The process of sex-stereotyping outlined earlier, whereby women are said to lack the key characteristics seen as essential in a manager, may be critical in promotion as well as in recruitment, so that once again women may be excluded.

Fourthly, women may be excluded from male-dominated social networks, membership of which are important in securing advancement in many organizations (Coe 1992: 15). Women may feel excluded from office conversations dominated by football and crude jokes, and managers and professionals have often met and done business on the golf course and in the bar, traditional male environments where some women may feel ill at ease.

Given that promotion decisions may be heavily influenced by the personal perceptions of those involved, there is always the risk that women will lose out in terms of promotion simply because senior managers know them less well, perhaps have an inaccurate view of their ambitions, and under-rate their job performance. This is particularly important in 'closed' promotion systems, where individuals are recommended for promotion by their superiors, rather than having to apply for internally advertised opportunities. This raises the question of the role of formal performance appraisal in promotion decisions.

Women managers and performance appraisal

For some, the lack of women managers in senior positions is due to:

the simple fact that the overwhelming majority of existing senior managers – who appraise the performance of subordinate female staff – are men. (Bennett 1986: 145)

On this view, women are caught in a 'catch 22' situation. They will not gain access to senior positions in large numbers until their performance and potential is fully recognized. This is most likely to occur where their performance is appraised by other women. However, senior management is dominated by men, who evaluate the performance of women managers from a male perspective, which reduces women's chances of promotion. Thus, what is needed if more women are to succeed is a larger number of successful women!

One possible way through this impasse would be to try to limit the potential for discrimination in performance appraisal – for example, by using behaviourally based appraisal scales, by training appraisers on the avoidance of sex-bias, and by making use of multiple raters in performance appraisal (Edwards and Cook 1985; Edwards and Sproull 1985; see chapter 3).

However, the evidence on sex-bias in performance appraisal is far from clear cut. Several studies have found little or no bias against women in performance appraisal ratings (Mobeley 1982; Wexley and Pulakos 1982; Peters et al. 1984; Bevan and Thompson 1992: 59–60). Such findings led one commentator to conclude that there is so little evidence of gender effects in formal performance appraisal systems that it 'is time to drop this line of research' (Latham 1986: 131).

This is not to suggest that there are no problems facing women managers in gaining access to senior managerial positions. On the contrary, given the small number of women in such positions, there appear to be very real problems. However, it may be that to try to reform the appraisal system is to address the wrong issue. Such an approach assumes that promotion decisions for managers are based on the rational outcomes of the formal appraisal process, so that all that is needed to create a 'level playing field' for women managers is the reform of this process.

In reality, promotion decisions are far less rational and mechanical than this, and the role of formal performance appraisal is often limited (see chapter 3). This would account for the lack of promotion of women managers on the one hand, and the apparent lack of evidence of a widespread and consistent gender bias in the formal appraisal process on the other. The forces standing in the way of greater numbers of women being promoted are complex and go beyond any possible bias in the formal appraisal process.

Why are there so few women managers? A summary

The above discussion suggests that the educational and career choices of women are not the only factors explaining their lack of career progress in management. The practices of employers and senior managers also play a role. Discrimination in recruitment and promotion decisions, the impact of women's domestic responsibilities, and the fact that employers traditionally determine their selection criteria and employment policies with a man in mind, all combine to disadvantage those women seeking a career in management.

Women as managers

Even when women break through into management they may face particular pressures simply because they are women. Women managers appear to suffer higher levels of stress than do male managers. This stems both from the domestic situation and from the work environment, with traditional gender stereotypes and discrimination each playing an important role.

Women managers tend not to receive the same level of domestic support from their spouse as is usual for male managers (Davidson and Cooper 1983). Even single women may suffer the disadvantage of domestic responsibilities, given that they are more likely than men to be expected to care for children and elderly relatives (Scase and Goffee 1989: 107–8).

Women have to face the common assumption that management is an essentially 'male' job, and in many cases the majority of their colleagues will be men. Thus, women managers have been characterized as 'travellers in a male world' (Marshall 1984). We have already examined the impact on recruitment and promotion, but there are also implications for women's day-to-day work experience.

Those women placed in the position of being amongst the first women managers in an organization may feel themselves to be under particular pressure to perform well, even to the extent of overachievement (Davidson and Cooper 1983). This is due to their high visibility within the organization, and because of a sense of being 'on trial' on behalf of women in general. As two recently appointed female managers put it to us:

> If we really had made a mess of it, there would have been a certain backtracking about putting women into managerial jobs.

> Other managers said 'You realize there will be a lot of people watching you, because if you make a mess of it they won't do it again' [appoint a woman manager].

Similar pressures are likely to exist wherever women are in a small minority. As we have seen, women managers may be excluded from informal social networks, leading to feelings of isolation. Furthermore, men may continue to view them according to traditional female stereotypes, often mistaking them for secretaries or assistants and expecting them to perform the role of corporate wives or mothers, for example by providing sympathetic counselling to their male colleagues (Scase and Goffee 1989).

Kanter (1977: 233–6) argues that women managers may be stereotyped in one of four ways: as 'mothers'; as the sex object or 'seductress'; as the vulnerable 'pet' who is patronized and in need of protection by her male colleagues; or as the 'iron maiden' who resists the other stereotypes and so is seen as a tough 'women's libber' by male colleagues, who keep their distance. Each of these stereotypes may harm women's careers, by undermining the quality of their work relationships and preventing them displaying the 'critical, independent, task-oriented behaviours' which are expected of male managers (Kanter 1977: 234).

Thus, even when a woman succeeds in securing a management job, she may face stresses and difficulties over and above those experienced by her male colleagues. It is hardly surprising that the proportion of women declines further up the management hierarchy.

What can employers do?

As argued at the beginning of this chapter, there are sound business reasons for employers to promote equal opportunities. In light of the difficulties faced by women in pursuing a managerial career, what can employers do to allow women to realize their managerial potential,

---

Box 7.3 Ten steps to a fairer workplace

In 1992, the UK Employment Department published a ten-point plan for employers. Approved by the Equal Opportunities Commission and the Commission for Racial Equality, the aim was to promote equal opportunities for women, ethnic minorities, older workers, people with disabilities, and ex-offenders. The ten points are:

1   Develop an equal opportunities policy covering recruitment, promotion and training.
2   Set an action plan, including targets.
3   Provide equal opportunities training for all.
4   Monitor the present position and progress in achieving objectives.
5   Review recruitment, selection, training and promotion procedures regularly.
6   Draw up clear and justifiable job criteria.
7   Offer pre-employment and positive action training.
8   Consider your organization's image.
9   Consider flexible working.
10   Develop links with local community groups, organizations and schools.

Source: *Employment Gazette*, April 1992: 143.
Crown Copyright. Reproduced with the permission of the Controller of Her Majesty's Stationery Office.

---

and in so doing also benefit the organization? The UK government has offered guidance for employers on equal opportunities. Box 7.3 outlines the Employment Department's ten-point plan.

By the late 1980s, there was evidence that British employers were introducing policies designed to recruit and retain women, largely in response to the decline in the number of young people entering the labour market (Lennon 1990). Box 7.4 outlines the main measures adopted by employers, according to a survey conducted in 1990.

Flexible working

The survey found that a majority of employers were taking steps either to recruit or retain women employees, the introduction of more flexible working patterns being the most widely used measure. This covers a variety of different practices, ranging from part-time working, through flexitime to telecommuting. Each of these provides

Box 7.4 Measures to recruit and retain women employees

Measure	percentage of organizations using the practice
Flexible working: flexible hours, part-time working, term-time working, homeworking/telecommuting, temporary working	76
Recruitment and selection measures: targeting job advertisements, targeting recruitment literature, training selectors in equal opps, using women interviewers	68
Consultation with women on changing employment practices	54
Job sharing	43
Extended maternity leave/enhanced benefits	42
Career-break schemes	32
Family leave	24
Childcare: workplace nurseries, childcare allowances or vouchers, after-school/ school holiday play schemes	23

Source: Industrial Relations Services, *Recruitment and Development Report*, 6, 19 June 1990: 4; based on a survey of 96 UK organizations conducted during 1990.

the employee with the opportunity to match the demands of the job with those of the home.

However, such working patterns have often been introduced for operational reasons, rather than specifically to promote equal opportunities for women. Part-time employees, in particular, have often been denied access to the full training and development opportunities enjoyed by their full-time colleagues, and have been largely restricted to lower-level jobs, with limited promotion prospects (Sidaway and Wareing 1992). The challenge facing employers is not simply to extend the scope for women to work flexible hours, but also to ensure that such options are available in higher-level jobs, and that such employees are afforded the opportunity to develop their skills and careers.

It may be difficult to provide part-time and flexible employment at the management level, given the requirement for many managerial jobs to be covered on a full-time basis (Sidaway and Wareing 1992). However, job sharing may offer a way round this problem. This differs from straightforward part-time working in that two employees share the responsibilities and rewards of a single job. Thus, the job can be covered on a full-time basis, and whilst there may be problems of consistency and coordination between the job sharers, these can be minimized by having handover periods when both are present. Job sharing may involve some increase in recruitment and training costs, but there is the advantage of being able to use the job share partner to cover for holidays and absences, and some employers have experienced lower absenteeism and labour turnover amongst job sharers (Incomes Data Services 1989).

Assistance with childcare

The provision by employers of childcare facilities is still patchy, in spite of some notable pioneering work, for example by the Midland Bank. In 1992 there were an estimated 425 workplace nurseries in the UK, providing 12,000 full-time day care places. Of these, 53 per cent were in the South-east of England, with Wales and Scotland accounting for only 4 and 3 per cent of nurseries respectively (*Industrial Relations Review and Report*, 508, March 1992: 3).

Many employers were deterred from providing workplace nurseries by the costs involved (Metcalf 1990). Initial set-up costs for a nursery are likely to be considerable, with estimates for 1990 ranging from £10,000 to £100,000 (Incomes Data Services 1990c). Furthermore, there is a need to secure planning permission for the buildings involved, and the approval of the local authority's social services department. Running costs are also high, with one estimate putting the annual running costs for a 25-place nursery at £100,000, or £4000 per place (Incomes Data Services 1990c). Even if an employer bears only a proportion of the costs, this may still represent a considerable addition to payroll costs.

Several employers have come to the view that nursery places are best provided on a community rather than a workplace basis. Particularly when commuting into large cities, parents often prefer nurseries near to the home rather than the workplace. For those employers with a scattered workforce, workplace provision is often not feasible. Thus, if employers are to play a direct role in the provision of childcare, the most likely option for most seems to be through joint schemes with other employers, particularly local authorities and other public-sector agencies, or through the purchase of places in existing nurseries (Incomes Data Services 1990c).

Childcare allowances or vouchers may provide a more flexible and cost-effective way of providing childcare assistance, particularly for smaller or multi-site employers. In the UK, Luncheon Vouchers supply 'childcare vouchers', which can be used to purchase childcare from a provider, who then redeems them from the issuing employer. Mercer Fraser offer 'childcare cheques', which are issued by the employer and can be paid directly into the employee's bank account. Even here, however, there may still be a problem for the employee in finding good quality childcare provision on which to spend the allowance or voucher.

Maternity leave and career breaks

Many employers have provided maternity leave conditions in excess of the statutory minimum in an attempt to retain female employees. Longer leave entitlement, higher maternity pay, the continuation of employment benefits during the leave period and the payment of return-to-work bonuses are amongst the measures taken (Industrial Relations Services 1990c).

Career breaks allow a longer period of time out than is provided for by maternity leave. Career breaks have been seen as a way of allowing women to maintain a degree of continuity in their career, whilst taking time out to have a family. They offer the employer an opportunity to retain scarce skills, particularly attractive where expensive training and development has been involved (Incomes Data Services 1991a).

Most schemes allow the employee to opt for a break of between two and five years, depending on their particular needs. During the break, the employee usually receives no remuneration or benefits, although there is an attempt to keep in touch, for example by sending out staff newsletters, inviting the individual to social events, nominating a particular employee to maintain contact, and perhaps by providing training courses or occasional days of employment (for which payment is made).

Those taking a career break are given some form of return-to-work promise. In some schemes, this involves a guarantee of re-employment, perhaps even into a supernumerary position if an established post is not immediately available. In others, the guarantee involves no more than a promise to place the returner on a reserve list, awaiting a suitable vacancy. Individuals will normally be required to give a period of notice of their wish to return to work of, for example, eight weeks.

Career-break schemes also vary in terms of eligibility criteria. Most schemes have a minimum service requirement, of anything up to five years, and in some cases eligibility is restricted to certain grades of staff. Thus, the scheme may be targeted at those with future career potential or scarce skills, although some employers have opted for wider eligibility so as not to appear divisive.

The 'family-friendly firm'

A key aim of many of the above initiatives was to adapt employment practices so that women, in particular, could more easily combine work with their domestic responsibilities. Some employers were developing these themes into 'family-friendly' employment policies, recognizing a need to address the non-work demands of both men and women employees. Whilst career-break schemes were designed primarily with women in mind, they are usually open to both sexes, and the IRS survey reported above showed that almost a quarter of those organizations questioned provided for employees of either sex to have time off to care for sick children or other dependents. Similarly, childcare facilities are made available to male and female employees.

The increase in the number of dual-career couples makes it likely that employers will need to adapt their employment policies accordingly. Assistance with spouse relocation will be a key area for many employers. A 1989 survey found that 73 per cent of employers felt that staff were reluctant to relocate because of working spouses. However, it also revealed that few employers had yet taken steps to deal with the issue, with only 9 per cent having a formal spouse relocation package as part of their relocation policy (Coe and Stark 1991: 11).

Assistance may take the form of financial compensation. For example, where a spouse gives up a job as part of a relocation, the relocating employer may pay the spouse's lost earnings for a period of perhaps six months. Some employers offer practical help in finding alternative employment for spouses, in some cases making direct offers of employment. However, whilst such policies may become increasingly necessary, they may not be sufficient to compensate a spouse for the disruption to a career and possible loss of promotion prospects. It may make more sense for employers to reconsider the necessity for employee mobility in the first place.

Reforming recruitment

As we saw earlier, the formalization of the recruitment and selection process can help minimize the risk of discrimination, by opening up the process to a wider range of applicants, by making selection criteria more explicit and by encouraging selectors to measure their decisions against job requirements. Some employers have gone further, adapting their recruitment and selection methods specifically to counter possible discrimination against women and actively encouraging women to apply for certain jobs.

This may involve the provision of equal opportunities training for interviewers; using more women interviewers; targeting job advertisements at women (for example, by placing them in media likely to be seen by women); and adapting recruitment brochures and advertisements to appeal specifically to women. Other initiatives include developing links with schools and colleges to try to encourage more girls to consider science and technology careers; holding open days; and providing pre-employment and assertiveness courses for women (Industrial Relations Services 1990b; Paddison 1990).

The Sex Discrimination Act allows employers to take steps to encourage either males or females to apply for a particular job, where that job has been done either entirely or mainly by members of one sex. However, the selection decision must be on merit, and employers must be careful not to give the impression that they have any intention of discriminating against members of either sex. Thus, in Britain the law draws a line between legal positive action and illegal positive discrimination. The position is similar with respect to ethnic minorities, and both the Equal Opportunities Commission and the Commission for Racial Equality have provided guidance for employers on positive action campaigns.

A good example of the positive action approach is provided by Prudential Assurance. Market research showed that around 90 per cent of its sales were either to women or were directly influenced by women, leading them to question the traditional assumption that the selling of insurance was best done by men. The traditional 'man from the Pru' image had deterred many women from applying for jobs, and the Prudential launched a targeted recruitment campaign, with advertisements featuring photographs of women and of ethnic minority workers, in an attempt to break down the white male stereotype. Initial experience at the Prudential and elsewhere suggests that such campaigns often produce greater numbers of applications from all groups, not just the ones being targeted – perhaps a result of the high profile and positive image which is thus created (Paddison 1990; Lennon 1990).

Some employers have also undertaken positive action on training, in an attempt to increase the numbers of women in management and in key technical specialisms. For example, the civil service has organized management training courses catering specifically for women, and Esso has run a management development course aimed at 'high-flying' women in their twenties. British Telecom, noting that women accounted for less than 3 per cent of the company's professional engineers, has experimented with a women-only conversion course, designed to prepare women for degree courses in engineering and information technology. The BBC has been a pioneer in women-only courses at both the managerial and non-managerial levels. The Corporation's 'Women's development programme', launched in May 1989, aims to help women in non-managerial jobs to realize their full potential. Renamed 'Springboard', the programme has been adopted by several other organizations in the UK (Arkin 1991b).

However, such examples are still rare and the numbers of women involved are small. Furthermore, such courses often appear marginal to the organization's mainstream training provision (Clarke 1991: 63–4). Even so, these courses may have a significance out of proportion to the numbers of women directly involved, in that they signal the organization's commitment to equal opportunities, and may encourage more women to aspire to managerial and technical careers.

Some organizations have identified targets for the recruitment and promotion of women and minorities (see box 7.5). Those adopting such targets argue that they promote equal opportunities and allow for the effective monitoring and evaluation of equal opportunities policies. In a few cases, organizations have linked managers' salaries or bonuses to the achievement of such equality targets, as for example at Grand Metropolitan. However, some organizations have rejected specific targets on the grounds that they might be taken to imply discrimination against men and the ethnic majority, which could deter such applicants, and which is illegal in the UK.

Box 7.5   On target for equal opportunities?

October 1991 saw the launch in the UK of 'Opportunity 2000', a campaign aimed at improving the employment and promotion prospects for women. Led by Business in the Community, a voluntary organization, and publicly launched by the Prime Minister, John Major, the campaign was in tune with the preferred voluntary approach of the government.

Organizations were invited to subscribe to the campaign by outlining the steps they would take to promote equal opportunities for women within their organization. By the launch date, 62 organizations had joined the campaign, including the BBC, British Airways, Grand Metropolitan, IBM (UK), ICI, the Metropolitan Police, NatWest Bank, Rank Xerox, Sainsbury's, Safeway, and the Kingfisher group, which includes B&Q, Woolworth, Comet and Superdrug. By May 1992, the number of participating organizations had grown to 110, including public- and private-sector organizations, and estimated by Business in the Community to account for 20 per cent of the UK workforce.

Organizations were free to determine their own approach. The BBC, for example, was to introduce additional measures on flexible working, and a policy on sexual harassment at work, and was to develop its equal opportunities monitoring procedures. The BBC aimed to increase the proportion of women in management and senior executive posts to 40 and 30 per cent respectively by 1996, with further targets to the year 2000.

The National Health Service established a central women's unit, to which health authorities and hospital trusts would have to report annually on their progress towards equal opportunities. Again, targets were set for the proportion of senior jobs to be held by women by 1994, and all short-lists for such jobs were to include female candidates. Where insufficient numbers of suitable women were applying for promotion, health authorities were required to identify and approach candidates from a list of women with promotion potential.

Sources: Financial Times, 29 October 1991: 10; 27 April 1992: 7; 6 May 1992: 10; *Employment Gazette*, December 1991: 637; *Guardian*, 9 January 1992: 18.

Have employers been doing enough?

Some commentators have argued that by the early 1990s, the response of UK employers was still limited. Ashburner (1991) argues that the introduction of such initiatives as improved maternity leave and childcare, whilst allowing more women to remain in employment, will not in itself overcome the crowding of women into lower-level jobs.

The NEDO/RIPA (1990: 70–2) report distinguishes between a 'life is work' approach and a 'life and work' approach by employers. The former involves helping women to meet the demands of an organizational career, for example by encouraging more women to enter traditionally male jobs and by offering assistance with childcare. The latter recognizes that traditional career patterns make unreasonable demands on women, and so involves a reassessment of careers – for example, by revising the requirements for long-term continuous employment and geographical mobility, by providing for longer career breaks, by making it easier for an individual to begin a managerial career later in life, and by redesigning jobs to allow greater job sharing and part-time working in more senior jobs.

The report argues that the more modest measures may fail to produce a major increase in the number of women managers, and that a more fundamental revision of employment practices is necessary if women are to make significant progress. This suggests that the organization must reassess its relationship with its employees, and increasingly recognize their non-work responsibilities and activities. This theme will be relevant to men as well as to women, if employees become more reluctant to subordinate their domestic and leisure interests to the pursuit of a career.

Women in management: The 1990s and beyond

To what extent are women likely to progress in management in the future? There is evidence that the number of women managers has been growing. The *Labour Force Survey* for Great Britain shows a rise in the proportion of managers who are women, up from under 21 per cent in 1979 to 28 per cent by 1990 (OPCS, various years).

In addition to measures aimed specifically at promoting equal opportunities, several other developments may be of benefit to women seeking a career in management. Greater employee involvement through initiatives such as TQM, and an apparent shift towards more open management styles in some organizations may mean that the traditional emphasis on the allegedly male characteristics of dominance, assertiveness and competitive individualism will decline. Many organizations are now emphasizing the need for greater communications and interpersonal skills amongst managers, including the ability to listen to the views of others (Rothwell 1985). We would not wish to substitute one managerial stereotype for another, but in some organizations at least it may become increasingly difficult to argue that management is a job demanding essentially 'male' characteristics (Hirsh and Jackson 1990: 31).

The trend towards greater flexibility in organizations may also benefit women. Market uncertainties have meant that the traditional hierarchical organization is in many cases being replaced with flatter organizational structures, with a greater use of short-term contracts and consultants, and less emphasis on the long-term continuous organizational career. Whilst such developments may bring greater insecurity for all staff, there are potential benefits for women, in that they may be better able to take career breaks without damaging their future prospects (Rothwell 1985; Nicholson and West 1988).

None of this is to suggest that the difficulties facing women have disappeared. The barriers which we have described in this chapter are in many organizations as serious as ever, and the Equal Opportunities Commission and others have called for changes in the legislation on equal pay and equal opportunities. Although many employers are confronting the issue of equal opportunities, the response is often piecemeal, and childcare is still a major problem for many women.

However, there does at least appear to be a growing awareness on the part of some employers that in the increasingly competitive environment of the 1990s, organizations cannot afford to go on underutilizing the potential of half the workforce, and many are now taking active steps to counter direct and indirect discrimination against women, and against other groups such as ethnic minorities, older people and people with disabilities. In this respect, the equal opportunities issue has become a key one for employers, and is likely to be at the heart of HRM developments in the future.

Summary and conclusions

In spite of the developments of recent years, women still face disadvantages relative to men in pursuing a career in management. In the earlier part of this chapter, we described the barriers faced by women, and we showed that even where they break through into management, women may still face particular difficulties and high levels of stress. In the latter part of the chapter, we described the steps which employers may take to promote equal opportunities. In many cases, these measures also apply to groups such as ethnic minorities, older workers and people with disabilities.

Rather than restate the full range of possible initiatives in this conclusion, we end with some general points of guidance. We suggest that organizations need to:

- Consider the importance of equal opportunities in terms of the effective recruitment, retention, utilization and motivation of high-quality employees, and in terms of sustaining a favourable corporate image.
- Establish an equal opportunities policy and identify clear responsibilities for the implementation and monitoring of the policy. Equal opportunities targets may be considered as part of this.
- Review the organization's employment policies and practices and consider their impact on equal opportunities and on the non-work lives of staff. This should include a review of all stages of the HRM cycle, from recruitment and selection, through appraisal, training and development, and rewards. Particular attention should be paid to the implicit assumptions underlying career patterns in the organization.
- Consider the implementation of a positive action campaign on recruitment, and on training and development.
- Implement equal opportunities training for managers and staff.

A key requirement of an effective approach is to avoid seeing equal opportunities as a stand-alone issue, which can be dealt with by one or two piecemeal initiatives. The message of research and good practice is that employers need a coordinated approach, which considers the equal opportunities implications of all aspects of HRM policy and practice, and which recognizes and reconciles the needs of both the organization and its staff.

Further reading

A useful guide for employers on equal opportunities is Helen Collins, *The Equal Opportunities Handbook: A Guide to Law and Best Practice in Europe*, Oxford: Blackwell, 1992. An interesting and insightful academic study of successful women entrepreneurs, managers, and professionals is Barbara White, Charles Cox and Cary Cooper, *Women's Career Development: A Study of High Fliers*, Oxford: Blackwell, 1992.

8
Conclusions

In this concluding chapter, we draw together some of the key themes to emerge from the earlier chapters, highlight some of the main developments in the management of managers, and suggest some ways forward.

We have argued that the performance of managers is critical in shaping the success of their own organizations and of the economy as a whole. The effective management of managers thus emerges as a key issue for senior executives, for managers themselves, and for all those concerned about the future performance of the economy. In fact, the concerns are not solely economic. The issues raised are of importance to all organizations, whether in the public, private or voluntary sectors, and the performance of managers impacts on all areas of our lives, as consumers, employees and as citizens.

We began the book with a review of some of the key factors affecting organizations and their managers. An increasingly uncertain environment means that many organizations are seeking to become less bureaucratic, more flexible, and more responsive to the needs of their customers or clients. Delayering has reduced the numbers of managers in many organizations. Those that remain are often less secure, and the predictable career path is for many a thing of the past.

All this has implications for managers. The greater emphasis on customer service and quality, and on initiatives such as TQM and the 'empowerment' of lower-level employees, mean that managerial decisions are placed under greater scrutiny from customers, both inside and outside the organization, and also from subordinates. In many organizations, there is a shift away from the notion of the manager as delegate or messenger; as simply passing down instructions from above. Whilst they are often taking on a broader range of technical functions, the role of managers as the only source of technical expertise and authority is being challenged. TQM and empowerment imply as much, in that all employees are encouraged to contribute to problem solving, on the assumption that management has no monopoly of technical knowledge. As organizations become more quality conscious, even the roles of troubleshooter and progress chaser, so long performed by many middle managers, may become less significant.

Thus, the manager's role is being transformed, particularly for those at middle-management level. The new role places greater emphasis on leadership, teambuilding, and the development and motivation of staff. Increasingly, managers are being expected to take greater responsibility for HR issues, including appraisal, development and rewards. All this demands new skills, many of them concerned with the management of people, rather than with technical production-related matters.

Given the scale and scope of such developments, it is hardly surprising that many have taken a pessimistic view of the future facing managers. Debates on the 'end of middle management' and the 'reluctant manager' have pointed to a decline in their numbers, with those remaining being placed under greater pressure; pressure which they are likely to resent. However, a counterargument has also been put forward, emphasizing the empowerment of managers themselves as a result of new technology, devolved authority and the encouragement of entrepreneurial risk-taking within organizations.

We have suggested that both the optimistic and pessimistic views contain an element of truth, but that organizations face important choices in the management of their managers, which can influence motivation and performance. However, we emphasize that there is not necessarily one best way to manage managers. Instead, the challenge is to find solutions which match the organization's internal and external environment and its strategy. In chapters 2 to 7, we examined the phases of the HRM cycle, in an attempt to show how organizations are meeting this challenge.

Chapter 2 showed that in spite of a tendency for practice to lag behind theory in recruitment and selection techniques, organizations are becoming more sophisticated in their approach to the recruitment and selection of managers. This is to be welcomed. Research has shown this to be a critical phase in the HRM cycle. Careful selection can pay dividends not only in terms of getting the right skills and experience, but also the right attitudes and commitment to the organization.

However, we would not recommend sophistication simply for its own sake. Psychometric testing and many of the other techniques referred to are, after all, expensive to use and can be counterproductive in untrained hands. There is a need to weigh up both benefits and costs. Organizations need to adopt a more informed approach to recruitment and selection, subjecting their approach to proper evaluation, and adapting it accordingly.

Chapter 3 showed how organizations are making increasing use of appraisal systems to meet multiple objectives, including not only the management of current performance, but also career and succession planning, management development and the management of longer-term performance. Whilst we have reservations about the use of a single appraisal system to meet potentially conflicting objectives, and about the tendency for formal appraisal to be ignored when it comes to promotion and development decisions, we feel that formal appraisal systems are likely to play an increasingly important role in managing managers in the flatter, more flexible, and performance-orientated organizations of the future.

However, consideration should be given to the use of appraisers other than simply the manager's immediate superior. The move towards more participative styles of management, with a greater emphasis on teamwork and a focus on customer requirements, means that the manager's subordinates, managerial colleagues and customers could make a useful input into the appraisal process, alongside the manager's boss. Once this is recognized, appraisal has the potential, in conjunction with rewards and development policies, to make a powerful contribution to the effective management of performance.

In chapter 4, we looked at management training and development. In spite of the UK's poor record by international standards, we found some evidence of a growth in the provision of training and development, both by business schools and by employers directly. It was encouraging to see that employers and managers are beginning to recognize the need for training and development to continue throughout a manager's career. However, many organizations still lack a systematic approach to the analysis of training needs, and training is all too often driven by fads rather than by individual and organizational needs.

Some employers are increasingly reluctant to send their managers on general open courses at business schools, and there has been a development of in-house provision of short courses, and of in-company MBAs. The work-based approach is taken to its logical conclusion in the Management Charter Initiative, which involves the assessment and development of management competencies at the workplace, though some organizations have developed their own competencies approach independently of the MCI. Such developments reflect a growing interest in training and development, with organizations seeking greater involvement in the design and delivery of training.

Chapter 5 dealt with career management, where the impact of the changing environment is perhaps most obvious. Many of the traditional approaches to career management have been based on the assumption of a relatively stable organization, with a hierarchical structure. Whilst there may be some merit in urging organizations to use the techniques of career and succession planning more systematically, there is clearly a need to think in terms of more flexible and unpredictable career structures. For many managers, it is time to jettison the notion of a career as climbing the organizational pyramid, and to think instead of lateral moves, of growth within the current job, and of inter-organizational mobility. For HRM policy-makers, the implication is that promotion can no longer necessarily be relied upon as the key motivator, and there is a need to think more creatively about career management. This has knock-on effects for most other aspects of HRM.

Chapter 6 dealt with remuneration policies, and two key themes emerged. Firstly, organizations are seeking to exploit the potential incentive effects of rewards, with an increasing use of performance-related pay, bonuses and share schemes. Secondly, whilst UK employers still generally offer less flexibility than those in the USA, there are signs that remuneration packages will be more flexible in future, perhaps even involving cafeteria benefits systems.

Both of these themes can be seen as an appropriate response to the challenges of the late twentieth century, as the bureaucratic approach to rewarding primarily on the basis of job size is increasingly irrelevant to organizational needs. With less scope to reward individuals by promotion, there is more emphasis on innovative approaches to rewarding performance in the current job. An increasingly diverse and demanding workforce also creates pressures to individualize remuneration packages.

Remuneration policy is in some organizations being seen as a means of managing performance and reinforcing corporate values through a coordinated range of incentives. Whilst the evidence on the direct incentive effects of remuneration is far from convincing, and the innovations in management remuneration often owed much to the recruitment and retention difficulties of the late 1980s, nevertheless many organizations appear committed to the goal of 'incentivization'. So long as remuneration planners focus on achieving longer-term changes in attitudes and behaviour, rather than simply looking for instant gains, we may expect such developments to produce tangible benefits.

Chapter 7 looked at equal opportunities, with a particular emphasis on the role of women. The under-representation of women in management is not simply a reflection of occupational choices and educational background. Organizational practices, particularly on selection and career management, also play an important role. Recent years have seen considerable interest in equal opportunities issues, not only for reasons of equity, but also because of a growing realization that equal opportunities makes good business sense. We showed how organizations may adapt their employment policies to promote equality of opportunity by allowing staff to accommodate domestic commitments more easily, and by confronting bias in the recruitment and selection process.

Whilst women and minorities still face barriers in the pursuit of a managerial career, and some have suggested that the response of many employers to equal opportunities is as yet piecemeal and uneven, it is encouraging to see equal opportunities issues being given such a high public profile. There is even a suggestion that more flexible employment policies, aimed initially at accommodating women, might herald a more 'family-friendly' firm as all employees, both male and female, are better able to balance their home and work commitments. Given the message of the 'reluctant manager' thesis on the increasing reluctance even of male managers to subordinate all to their careers, such issues are likely to remain on the corporate agenda in the years to come.

We saw in the introductory chapter that there has been a tendency in some organizations to assume that managers are 'self-starters', who need little guidance or feedback from their seniors, and are best left to 'sink or swim' by their own efforts (Longenecker and Gioia 1991). Many of the developments which we have described in this book are consistent with a more effective management of managers, although it appears that not all organizations are yet innocent of practising the 'sink or swim' approach. For example, management training and development is still often *ad hoc* and inadequate, and many managers still express concern about the ineffectiveness of appraisal systems and the limited attention given to career management. Thus, whilst we see some encouraging signs, there is clearly still some way to go in many organizations.

A common thread running through the book is that organizations need to take a strategic approach to the management of their managers. There are two issues here. Firstly, HRM policies need to be consistent with, and indeed contribute towards, the achievement of organizational goals. We have found some evidence to suggest that those responsible for the management of managers are beginning to recognize this, and we have tried to show how this can be achieved.

Secondly, HRM policies must themselves be consistent, and contribute towards an integrated approach to the management of managers. We have emphasized that no individual initiative or technique can be seen as a quick-fix solution. What counts is a coordinated approach to resourcing, development and the management of performance. Performance-related pay, for example, if it is to amount to anything more than simply throwing money at staff, must form part of a wider package of measures designed to address questions of training and development, management style and communications.

The need for consistency between the various elements of the HRM cycle is a critical, but often neglected, notion. HR policies necessarily contain basic assumptions about individual motivation and behaviour, and about the management style of the organization. However, it is not uncommon to find HR policies within an organization based on conflicting assumptions, with the risk that such policies will fail to have their intended effect.

For example, a remuneration policy based on rewarding individual effort, tied to short-term financial targets, is based on particular assumptions about individual motivation and behaviour, and about the appropriate management style. This could clash with an attempt to develop a more cooperative, team-based approach, or with the encouragement of long-term development through an open appraisal system. The latter may be based on the assumption that what motivates people is rewarding work relationships and long-term development opportunities. Were such policies to be implemented in the same organization, the individual manager would be likely to experience conflicting signals as to what is the appropriate behaviour. At least some of the policies are likely to fail, and there is a risk of underperformance.

The problem is that HR policies are often developed in relative isolation from one another, in response to particular problems. Devanna et al. (1984), in their discussion of strategic HRM, suggest that if top management is to avoid such pitfalls, they need to consider several basic dimensions in designing their HR systems (see box 8.1), and to ensure that the overall approach to HR is consistent.

Box 8.1 Dimensions to consider in the design of HR systems

HR systems can be considered along the following dimensions:

Nature of the employment contract

What is the nature of the 'psychological contract' between the organization and its employees?

Fair day's work for a fair ⟵————————⟶ Challenging, meaningful
day's pay   work in return for loyal,
                                                committed service

Degree of participation in decision making

Do most initiatives come from the top, or are those at lower levels involved in the decision making process?

Top-down ⟵————————⟶ Bottom-up

Internal versus external labour markets

To what extent does the organization rely on promotion from within?

Hire from external ⟵————————⟶ Promote mainly
labour market   from within

Group versus individual performance

To what extent is the emphasis on teamwork or on individual effort?

Group/team-based effort ⟵————————⟶ Individual effort seen
seen as critical   as critical

Source: Developed from Devanna et al., 1984: 37–41.

The list is not necessarily exhaustive, but the point is that there is a need to think strategically, and to develop a holistic view of the HR cycle to ensure consistency and fit.

As should by now be clear, many of the current trends in management practice contain potential contradictions. For example, both total quality management (TQM) and performance-related pay (PRP) became increasingly popular during the 1980s and early 1990s. However, Deming, one of the American quality gurus and a key figure in the TQM movement, has argued that PRP is incompatible with TQM, and in particular that to pay individuals for quality actually risks undermining their commitment to quality, and instead fosters a crude instrumentalism. Quality experts such as Crosby argue that what is important to employees is recognition, rather then cash, and that an appropriate approach is symbolic reward, such as praise and public accolades (Drummond and Chell 1992).

Of course, this ignores the fact that PRP might itself be seen as a form of recognition (see chapter 6), but the point is that there are possible tensions between the various developments in management practice. This is all the more reason to avoid faddism and a search for *ad hoc*, quick-fix solutions to particular problems, and instead to look for the consistency of approach which we are describing.

How is the management of managers likely to develop in the future? It is always tempting to read current developments as indicative of longer-term trends, but prediction is a hazardous occupation and it is appropriate to sound a note of caution. The more widespread use of sophisticated selection techniques and performance-related pay, and the adoption of women-friendly employment policies, were to some extent driven by the recruitment and retention difficulties of the late-1980s boom. The recession of the early 1990s did appear to check the growth in employer provision of childcare facilities, and there were some signs of disillusionment with performance-related rewards in a period of declining corporate performance. However, we have tried to demonstrate that most of the initiatives described in this book are a response to the longer-term developments in the corporate environment. As such they should outlast any economic downturn. Only time will tell.

Bibliography

Adshead, John 1990: Headhunting without tears. *Personnel Management*, October, 56–7.

Advertising Association 1990: *Annual Report*. London: Advertising Association.

Akande, Adebowale 1992: One more time: The mentor connection. *Equal Opportunities International*, 11, 4, 6–8.

Alban-Metcalfe, Beverley 1989: *The Uses of Assessment Centres in the NHS*. London: NHS Training Agency.

Alban-Metcalfe, Beverley and Nicholson, Nigel 1984: *The Career Development of British Managers*. London: British Institute of Management.

Alford, B. W. E. 1988: *British Economic Performance, 1945–1975*. London: Macmillan.

Alimo-Metcalfe, Beverley 1992: Appraisal appraised: Lessons from the NHS. *Local Government*, Autumn, 18–19.

Allen, Thomas and Katz, Ralph 1986: The dual ladder: Motivational solution or managerial delusion? *R&D Management*, 16, 185–97.

Anderson, Alan H. 1992: *Successful Training Practice: A Manager's Guide to Personnel Development*. Oxford: Blackwell.

Anderson, Neil and Shackleton, Vivian 1990: Staff selection decision making into the 1990s. *Management Decision*, 28, 1, 5–8.

Anon 1981: Headhunting: How the executive search game is played. *Personnel Executive*, September, 28–31.

Arkin, Anat 1990: Cutting out the middle manager. *Personnel Management Plus*, 1, 3, September, 16–17.

Arkin, Anat 1991a: Managing to give a good local service. *Personnel Management*, September, 49–51.

Arkin, Anat 1991b: A springboard to equal opportunities. *Personnel Management*, February, 57–8.

Armstrong, Michael and Murlis, Helen 1991: *Reward Management: A Handbook of Remuneration Strategy and Practice*. Second edition. London: Kogan Page.

Ashburner, L. 1991: Men managers and women workers: Women employees as an under-used resource. *British Journal of Management*, 2, 3–15.

Ashton, David 1988: Are business schools good learning organizations? Institutional values and their effects in management education. *Personnel Review*, 17, 4, 9–14.

Ashton, David 1989: The case for tailor made MBAs. *Personnel Management*, July, 32–5.

Ashworth, Ian and Associates 1988: *A Study of Industry's Use of Headhunting*. London.

Bailyn, L. 1980: *Living with Technology: Issues at Mid-Career*. Cambridge, Mass.: MIT Press.

Bain, G. 1992: Overseas ventures. *The Times Higher Education Supplement*, 11 September, 22.

Bamber, Greg 1986: *Militant Managers? Managers' Unionism and Industrial Relations*. Aldershot: Gower.

Barber, Alison E., Dunham, Randall B., and Formisano, Roger A. 1992: The impact of flexible benefits on employee satisfaction: A field study. *Personnel Psychology*, 45, 55–75.

Barlow, Graham 1989: Deficiencies and the perpetuation of power: latent functions in management appraisal. *Journal of Management Studies*, 26, 499–517.

Barrow, Simon 1990: *Turning recruitment advertising into a competitive weapon*. Paper given at the IPM National Conference, Harrogate.

Baughman, James 1988: In Reibstein, Larry, Firms ask workers to rate their bosses. *Wall Street Journal*, 13 June, 19.

Beaumont, Stella 1989: Why today's workers are on the move. *Personnel Management*, April, 42–6.

Beilinson, Jerry 1990: Under surveillance. *Personnel*, December, 3–4.

Bennett, Roger 1986: How performance appraisals hurt women managers. *Women in Management Review*, Autumn, 145–53.

Bennison, Malcolm and Casson, Jonathan 1984: *The Manpower Planning Handbook*. London: McGraw-Hill.

Bernardin, John and Klatt, Lawrence 1985: Managerial appraisal systems: Has practice caught up to the state of the art? *Personnel Administrator*, 30, 11, 79–86.

Bevan, Stephen and Fryatt, Julie 1988: *Employee Selection in the UK*. Brighton: Institute of Manpower Studies.

Bevan, Stephen and Thompson, Marc 1991: Performance management at the crossroads. *Personnel Management*, November, 36–9.

Bevan, Stephen and Thompson, Marc 1992: *Merit Pay, Performance Appraisal and Attitudes to Women's Work*, IMS Report No. 234, Institute of Manpower Studies, Brighton.

Bishop, James 1989: The executive search for ethical character. *Directors and Boards*, Spring, 21–4.

Blanksby, Margaret and Iles, Paul 1990: Recent developments in assessment centre theory, practice and operation. *Personnel Review*, 19, 6, 33–43.

Blinkhorn, Steve 1991: *Uses and Abuses of Psychological Tests*. Paper given at the IPM National Conference, Harrogate.

Blinkhorn, Steve and Johnson, Charles 1990: The insignificance of personality testing. *Nature*, 348, December, 671–2.

Boak, George 1991: *Developing Managerial Competencies*. London: Pitman.

Bogan, Paulette 1990: Rent-a-head. *Personnel*, 67, November, 10.

Brewster, Chris 1988: *The Management of Expatriates*, Human Resources Research Centre Monograph no. 2, Cranfield: The Cranfield School of Management.

Burgoyne, John 1989: Creating the managerial portfolio: Building on competency approaches to management. *Management Education and Development*, 20, 1, 56–61.

Bush, Gerald and Stinson, John 1980: A different use of performance appraisal: Evaluating the boss. *Management Review*, November, 14–17.

Business Council of Australia 1990: *Training Australians. A Better Way of Working*. Melbourne: BCA.

Campbell-Johnston, George 1983: Recruitment of experienced managers. In B. Ungerson (ed.), *Recruitment Handbook*. Third Edition. Aldershot: Gower.

Cannell, Michael and Wood, Stephen 1992: *Incentive Pay: Impact and Evolution*. London: IPM.

Cederbloum, D. and Lounsboury, J. W. 1980: An investigation of user acceptance of peer evaluations. *Personnel Psychology*, 33, 567–79.

Chalkey, Peter 1981: Quoted in: Headhunting: How the executive search game is played. *Personnel Executive*, September, 28–9.

City Research Associates 1988: *The Price Waterhouse Recruitment Advertising Survey*. London: Price Waterhouse.

Clark, Ian and Clark, Tim 1990: Personnel management and the use of executive recruitment consultancies. *Human Resource Management Journal*, 1, 1, 46–62.

Clark, Tim 1989: *The Executive Search and Selection Industry: An Analysis of an Emerging Industry*. Leicester: Leicester Business School.

Clarke, Karen 1991: *Women and Training: A Review*. Equal Opportunities Commission, Research Discussion Series No. 1.

Clutterbuck, David 1985: *Everyone needs a mentor*. London: Institute of Personnel Management.

Coe, Trudy 1992: *The Key to the Men's Club: Opening the Doors to Women in Management*. London: Institute of Management.

Coe, Trudy and Stark, Andrew 1991: *On the Move: Manager Mobility in the 1990s*. London: British Institute of Management.

Colgan, Fiona and Tomlinson, Frances 1991: Women in publishing: Jobs or careers? *Personnel Review*, 20, 5, 16–26.

Collinson, David 1991: 'Poachers turned gamekeepers': Are personnel managers one of the barriers to equal opportunities? *Human Resource Management Journal*, 1, 3, Spring, 58–76.

Collinson, David, Knights, David and Collinson, Margaret 1990: *Managing to Discriminate*. London: Routledge.

Constable, J. and McCormick, R. 1987: *The Making of British Managers*. London: British Institute of Management and Confederation of British Industry.

Cowling, Alan and Walters, Mike 1990: Manpower planning – Where are we today? *Personnel Review*, 19, 3, 3–8.

Creelman, James 1991: Upwards Appraisal at AMEX and BP. *The Mentor*, 1, 2, 12.

Crofts, Pauline 1992: Outplacement: A way of never having to say you're sorry? *Personnel Management*, May, 46–50.

Curnow, Barry 1986: The creative approach to pay. *Personnel Management*, October, 70–5.

Curnow, Barry 1989: Recruit, retrain, retain: Personnel management and the three R's. *Personnel Management*, November, 40–7.

Curran, Margaret M. 1988: Gender and recruitment: People and places in the labour market. *Work, Employment and Society*, 2, 3, September, 335–51.

Davidson, Marilyn and Cooper, Cary 1983: *Stress and the Woman Manager*. Oxford: Martin Robertson.

Davies, John and Deighan, Yvonne 1986: The managerial menopause. *Personnel Management*, March, 28–32.

Delahaye, Brian 1992: A theoretical context of management development and education. In Barry J. Smith (ed.), *Management Development in Australia*. Sydney: Harcourt Brace Jovanovich, 1–18.

Devanna, Mary Anne, Fombrun, Charles J. and Tichy, Noel M. 1984: A framework for strategic human resource management. In Fombrun, Charles J., Tichy, Noel M., and Devanna, Mary Anne (eds), *Strategic Human Resource Management*. New York: Wiley, 33–51.

Dex, Shirley 1984: *Women's Work Histories: An Analysis of the Women and Employment Survey*. Department of Employment Research Paper No. 46.

Dopson, Sue and Stewart, Rosemary 1990: What *is* happening to middle management? *British Journal of Management*, 1, 1, April, 3–16.

Dowling, Peter J. and Schuler, Randall S. 1990: *International Dimensions of Human Resource Management*, Boston, Mass: PWS-Kent.

Drucker, Peter F. 1987: *The Frontiers of Management*. London: Heinemann.

Drummond, Helga and Chell, Elizabeth 1992: Should organizations pay for quality? *Personnel Review*, 21, 4, 3–11.

Dulewicz, Victor 1991: Improving assessment centres. *Personnel Management*, 23, 6, 50–5.

Edwards, Mark and Cook, Suzanne 1985: Team Evaluation. *Women in Management Review*, Autumn, 168–71.

Edwards, Mark and Sproull, J. 1985: Making performance appraisals perform: The use of team evaluation. *Personnel*, March.

Equal Opportunities Commission 1991: *Men and Women in Britain*. London: HMSO.

ER Consultants 1992: *Who's Managing the Managers? The Reward and Career Development of Middle Managers in a Flat Organisation*. London: Institute of Management.

Evans, Paul 1986: New directions in career management. *Personnel Management*, 18, 12, 26–9.

Evans, Paul 1990: International management development and the balance between generalism and professionalism. *Personnel Management*, 22, 12, 46–50.

Falconer, Heather 1991: Number games. *Personnel Today*, October, 29.

Finn, R. H. and Fontaine, P. A. 1983: Performance appraisal: Some dynamics and dilemmas. *Public Personnel Management Journal*, 13, 4, 335–43.

Fletcher, Clive 1986: Should the test score be kept a secret? *Personnel Management*, April, 44–6.

Fletcher, Clive 1987: The effects of performance review in appraisal: Evidence and implications. *Journal of Management Development*, 5, 3, 3–12.

Fletcher, Clive, Blinkhorn, Steve and Johnson, Charles 1991: Personality tests: The great debate. *Personnel Management*, September, 38–42.

Fombrun, Charles and Laud, Robert 1983: Strategic issues in performance appraisal: Theory and practice. *Personnel*, November–December, 23–31.

Fordham, K. G. 1983: Job Advertising. In Bernard Ungerson (ed.), *Recruitment Handbook*. Third edition. Aldershot: Gower, 46–63.

Fowler, Alan 1988: New directions in performance pay. *Personnel Management*, November, 30–4.

Fuller, Linda and Smith, Vicki 1991: Consumers' reports: Management by customers in a changing economy. *Work, Employment, and Society*, 5, 1, 1–16.

Gabris, Gerald and Rock, Steven 1991: Situational interviews and job performance: The results in one public agency. *Public Personnel Management*, 20, 4, 469–83.

George, Claude Jr. 1972: *The History of Management Thought*. Englewood Cliffs: Prentice-Hall.

Gill, Deirdre 1977: *Appraising performance: Present Trends and The Next Decade*. London: Institute of Personnel Management.

Gill, Deirdre 1980: *Selecting Managers: How British Industry Recruits*. London: British Institute of Management.

Goffee, Robert and Scase, Richard 1986: Are the rewards worth the effort? Changing managerial values in the 1980s. *Personnel Review*, 15, 4, 3–6.

Goodswen, Michael 1988: Retention and reward of the high achiever. *Personnel Management*, October, 61–4.

Grant, Peter and Holmes, J. D. 1991: Putting professionals and managers on equal footing. *Personnel*, July, 17–18.

Gratton, Lynda and Syrett, Michel 1990: Heirs apparent: Succession strategies for the future. *Personnel Management*, 22, 1, 34–8.

Guardian 1988: *Why Work?* London: Guardian.

Hales, Colin P. 1986: What do managers do? A critical review of the evidence. *Journal of Management Studies*, 23, 1, January, 88–115.

Hall, D. T. 1976: *Careers in Organizations*. Los Angeles: Goodyear.

Handy, Charles 1987: *The Making of Managers: A Report on Management Training, Education and Development in the United States, West Germany, France, Japan and the UK*. London: NEDO.

Handy, Charles, Gordon, Colin, Gow, Ian and Randlesome, Collin 1988: *Making Managers*. London: Pitman.

Hanson, Charles G. 1991: *Taming the Trade Unions: A Guide to the Thatcher Government's Employment Reforms, 1980–90*. London: Macmillan.

Heneman, Robert L. 1992: *Merit Pay: Linking Pay Increases to Performance Ratings*. Reading, Mass.: Addison Wesley.

Herriot, Peter 1989: *Recruitment in the 90s*. London: Institute of Personnel Management.

Herriot, Peter and Fletcher, Clive 1990: 'Candidate friendly' selection for the 1990s. *Personnel Management*, February, 32–5.

Herriot, Peter and Pinder, Rob 1992: HR strategy in a changing world. *Personnel Management*, August, 36–9.

Herzberg, Frederick, Mausner, Bernard and Snyderman, Barbara Bloch 1959: *The Motivation to Work*. Second edition. New York: Wiley.

Hill, J. R. W. and Maycock, A. B. 1991: *The Design of Recruitment Advertisements Featuring Questions which have a Thematic Content*. Paper presented at the Occupational Psychology Conference.

Hirsh, Wendy 1990: *Succession Planning: Current Practice and Future Issues*. IMS Report No. 184, Brighton: Institute of Manpower Studies.

Hirsh, W. and Bevan, S. 1988: *What Makes a Manager? In Search of a Language for Management Skills*. IMS Report No. 105, Brighton: Institute of Manpower Studies.

Hirsh, Wendy and Jackson, Charles 1990: *Women Into Management: Issues Influencing the Entry of Women Into Management Jobs*. IMS Report No. 158, Brighton: Institute of Manpower Studies.

Hogg, Clare 1988a: *Outdoor Training*. Personnel Management Factsheet, No. 9.

Hogg, Clare 1988b: *MBAs*. Personnel Management Factsheet, No. 12.

Hogg, Clare 1989: Executives for hire. *Director*, October, 134–8.

Holden, Len 1991: European trends in training and development. *International Journal of Human Resource Management*, 2, 113–31.

Holden, Nigel 1990: Preparing the ground for organizational learning: Graduate training programmes in major Japanese corporations. *Management Education and Development*, 21, 3, 241–61.

Holland, John 1973: *Making Vocational Choices: A Theory of Careers*. Englewood Cliffs, NJ: Prentice-Hall.

Howard, Ann 1974: An assessment of assessment centers. *Academy of Management Journal*, 17, 115–34.

Hunt, John 1986: Alienation among managers – The new epidemic or the social scientists' invention? *Personnel Review*, 15, 1, 21–6.

Hunt, David and Michael, Carol 1983: Mentorship: A career training and development tool. *Academy of Management Review*, 8, 3, 475–85.

Iles, Paul 1989: Using assessment and development centres to facilitate equal opportunity in selection and career development. *Equal Opportunities International*, 8, 5, 1–26.

Incomes Data Services 1989: Job sharing. *IDS Study*, 440, August.

Incomes Data Services 1990a: *Recruiting Managers and Professionals*. London: IDS Top Pay Unit.

Incomes Data Services 1990b: *Putting Pay Philosophies into Practice*. London: IDS Top Pay Unit.

Incomes Data Services 1990c: Childcare. *IDS Study*, 472, December.

Incomes Data Services 1991a: Maternity leave and career breaks. *IDS Study*, 476, February.

Incomes Data Services 1991b: Bonus schemes, Part 2. *IDS Study*, 492, October.

Incomes Data Services 1992: *Cars or Cash*. London: IDS Top Pay Unit.

Incomes Data Services no date: *A Guide to Performance Related Pay*. London: IDS Public Sector Unit.

Industrial Relations Services 1990a: Recruiting and retaining women workers: 1 – The most effective methods. *Recruitment and Development Report*, 6, 19 June, 2–5.

Industrial Relations Services 1990b: Recruiting and retaining women workers: 2 – Employers meet the challenge. *Recruitment and Development Report*, 7, 17 July, 2–9.

Industrial Relations Services 1990c: Recruiting and retaining women workers: 3 – A workforce with domestic responsibilities. *Recruitment and Development Report*, 8, 21 August, 2–10.

Industrial Relations Services 1991a: The state of selection. *Recruitment Report*, 16, 17 and 19.

Industrial Relations Services 1991b: Executive recruitment: A case for using your headhunter? *Recruitment and Development Report*, 24, 2–11.

Industrial Relations Services 1991c: Developing managers in the great outdoors. *Recruitment and Development Report*, 14, 6–9.

Industrial Relations Services 1991d: Qualifications for managers. The quiet revolution? *Recruitment and Development Report*, 22, 2–9.

Industrial Relations Services 1991e: BT managers hostile to performance-related pay. *IRS Employment Trends*, 6 September, 2–3.

Industrial Relations Services 1992: The role of outdoor-based development: A survey of 120 employers. *Employee Development Bulletin*, 34, 2–17.

James, K. M. 1989: A case of the emperor's clothes. *Training and Development*, October, 18.

Johnston, Julia 1991: An empirical study of the repatriation of managers in UK multinationals. *Human Resource Management Journal*, 1, 4, Summer, 102–9.

Jones, Rob 1990: Integrating selection in a merged company. *Personnel Management*, September, 38–42.

Kane, Jeffrey and Lawler, Edward 1978: Methods of Peer Assessment. *Psychological Bulletin*, 85, 555–86.

Kanter, Rosabeth Moss 1977: *Men and Women of the Corporation*. New York: Basic Books.

Kanter, Rosabeth Moss 1990: *When Giants Learn to Dance: Mastering the Challenges of Strategy, Management and Careers in the 1990s*. London: Unwin Paperbacks.

Kay, E., Meyer, H. H. and French, J. R. P. 1965: Effects of threat in a performance appraisal interview. *Journal of Applied Psychology*, 49, 311–17.

Kessler, Ian and Purcell, John 1992: Performance related pay: Objectives and application. *Human Resource Management Journal*, 2, 3, Spring, 16–33.

Kingston, Neil 1971: *Selecting Managers*. London: British Institute of Management.

Knights, David and Raffo, Carlo 1990: Milkround professionalism in personnel recruitment: Myth or reality. *Personnel Review*, 19, 1, 28–37.

Kotter, John 1982: *The General Managers*. New York: Free Press.

Kotter, John 1990: *A Force for Change: How Leadership Differs from Management*. New York: The Free Press.

KPMG Peat Marwick Management Consultants/Institute of Personnel Management 1990: *Age has its Compensations*. KPMG Peat Marwick Management Consultants/IPM.

Kubr, Milan and Prokopenko, Joseph 1989: *Diagnosing Management Training and Development Needs*. Geneva: ILO.

Latham, Gary 1986: Job performance and appraisal. In Cary Cooper and Ivan Robertson (eds), *International Review of Industrial and Organisational Psychology*. Chichester: Wiley, 117–55.

Legge, Karen 1978: *Power, Innovation and Problem Solving in Personnel Management*. Maidenhead: McGraw-Hill.

Lennon, Pat 1990: Facing the demographic challenge. *Employment Gazette*, January, 41–4.

Levinson, D. J., Darrow, C. N., Klein, E. B., Levinson, M. H. and

McKee, B. 1978: *The Seasons of a Man's Life.* Alfred A. Knopf: New York.

Long, Phil 1986: *Performance Appraisal Revisited.* London: Institute of Personnel Management.

Long, George and Tonks, David 1991: *The Hidden Rhetoric of Competition in the Marketing Game.* Proceedings of Marketing in Education Group Conference, Cardiff Business School, 2, 646–69.

Longenecker, Clinton and Gioia, Dennis 1988: Neglected at the top – executives talk about executive appraisal. *Sloan Management Review,* Winter, 41–7.

Longenecker, Clinton, and Gioia, Dennis 1991: SMR Forum: Ten myths of managing managers. *Sloan Management Review,* Fall, 81–90.

Longenecker, Clinton, Sims, Henry Jr., and Gioia, Dennis 1987: Behind the mask: The politics of employee appraisal. *Academy of Management Executive,* 1, 3, 183–93.

Lowe, James 1991: Teambuilding via outdoor training: Experiences from a UK automotive plant. *Human Resource Management Journal,* 1, 2, 42–59.

Lunn, Terry 1987: A scientific approach to successful selection. *Personnel Management,* December, 43–5.

Mabey, Bill 1989: The majority of large companies use occupational tests. *Guidance and Assessment Review,* 5, 3, 2–4

Macdonell, Richard 1989: Management by Objectives. In Peter Herriot (ed.), *Assessment and Selection in Organizations.* Chichester: Wiley, 701–10.

McEvoy, Glen and Beatty, Richard 1989: Assessment centres and subordinate appraisals of managers: A seven-year examination of predictive validity. *Personnel Psychology,* 42, 37–52.

McEvoy, Glen and Buller, Paul 1987: User acceptance of peer appraisals in an industrial setting. *Personnel Psychology,* 40, 785–97.

McGuire, Peter 1980: Why performance appraisals fail. *Personnel Journal,* September, 744–62.

Mackay, Lesley and Torrington, Derek 1986: *The Changing Nature of Personnel Management.* London: Institute of Personnel Management.

McKinlay, Alan and Starkey, Ken 1992: Competitive strategies and organizational change. In Graeme Salaman (ed.), *Human Resource Strategies.* London: Sage, 107–23.

Maclagan, Patrick 1990: Moral behaviour in organizations: the contribution of management education and development. *British Journal of Management,* 1, 1, 17–26

Maclagan, Patrick and Snell, Robin 1992: Some implications for management development of research into managers' moral dilemmas. *British Journal of Management,* 3, 157–68.

Mahoney, Thomas A. 1992: Multiple pay contingencies: Strategic design of compensation. In Graeme Salaman (ed.), *Human Resource Strategies.*

London: Sage, 337–46.

Main, Brian and Johnston, James 1992: Deciding on top pay by committee. *Personnel Management*, July, 32–5.

Malloch, Hedley 1988: Evaluating strategies on a cost-based manpower planning model. *Personnel Review*, 17, 3, 22–8.

Mansfield, Roger and Poole, Michael 1991: *British Management in the Thatcher Years*. London: British Institute of Management.

Mant, Alistair 1977: *The Rise and Fall of the British Manager*. London: Macmillan.

Marchington, Mick, Goodman, John, Wilkinson, Adrian, and Ackers, Peter 1992: *New Developments in Employee Involvement*, Research Series No. 2, Employment Department, May.

Marsden, David and Richardson, Ray 1991: *Does Performance Pay Motivate? A Study of Inland Revenue Staff*. London: Inland Revenue Staff Federation, quoted in Cannell and Wood (1992).

Marshall, Judi 1984: *Women Managers: Travellers in a Male World*. Chichester: Wiley.

Martin, Bob 1987: Recruitment ad ventures. *Personnel Journal*, August, 46–63.

Maurier, Steven and Fay, Charles 1988: Effect of situational interviews, conventional structured interviews, and training on interview rating agreement: An experimental analysis. *Personnel Psychology*, 41, 329–44.

Mayo, Andrew 1991: *Managing Careers: Strategies for Organizations*. London: Institute of Personnel Management.

Metcalf, Hilary 1990: *Retaining Women Employees: Measures Designed to Counteract Labour Shortages*. IMS Report No. 190, Brighton: Institute of Manpower Studies.

Meyer, Herbert 1980: Self-appraisal of job performance. *Personnel Psychology*, 33, 291–5.

Meyer, Herbert H., Kay, Emanuel and French, John R. P. 1965: Split Roles in Performance Appraisal. *Harvard Business Review*, 43, 123–9.

Miles, Raymond E. and Snow, Charles C. 1978: *Organizational Strategy, Structure and Process*. New York: McGraw-Hill.

Mintzberg, Henry 1983: *Structure in Fives: Designing Effective Organizations*. Englewood Cliffs, N.J.: Prentice Hall.

Mobeley, W. H. 1982: Supervisor and employee race and sex effects on performance appraisals: A field study of adverse impact and generalizability. *Academy of Management Journal*, 25, 598–606.

Mumford, Alan 1989: *Management Development: Strategies for Action*. London: Institute of Personnel Management.

Mumford, John and Buley, Tony 1988: Rewarding behavioural skills as part of performance. *Personnel Management*, December, 33–7.

Murlis, Helen and Fitt, David 1991: Job evaluation in a changing world. *Personnel Management*, May, 39–43.

Murlis, Helen and Pritchard, Derek 1991: The computerised way to evaluate jobs. *Personnel Management*, April, 48–53.

National Economic Development Office/Royal Institute of Public Administration (NEDO/RIPA) 1990: *Women Managers: The Untapped Resource*. London: NEDO/RIPA.

Newstrom, John, Lengnick-Hall, Mark and Rubenfeld, Steven 1987: How employees can choose their own bosses. *Personnel Journal*, December, 121–6.

Nicholson, Nigel 1987: Work-role transitions: Processes and outcomes. In Peter Warr (ed.), *Psychology at Work*. Third edition. Harmondsworth, Middlesex: Penguin, 160–77.

Nicholson, Nigel and West, Michael A. 1988: *Managerial Job Change: Men and Women in Transition*. Cambridge: Cambridge University Press.

Nolan, Peter 1989: The productivity miracle? In Francis Green (ed.), *The Restructuring of the UK Economy*. London: Harvester Wheatsheaf, 101–21.

Odiorne, George 1984: *Strategic Management of Human Resources: A Portfolio Approach*. San Francisco: Jossey Bass.

Odiorne, George 1990: The trend to quarterly performance review. *Business Horizons*, 33, July–August, 38–41.

O'Driscoll, Michael, and Taylor, Paul 1992: Congruence between theory and practice in management training needs analysis. *International Journal of Human Resource Management*, 3, 3, 575–84.

Olin, Judy D. and Rynes, Sara L. 1984: Organizational staffing: integrating practice with strategy. *Industrial Relations*, 23, 2, Spring, 170–83.

Office of Population Censuses and Surveys various years: *Labour Force Survey*. London: HMSO.

Ornstein, Suzyn, Cron, William L. and Slocum, John W. 1989: Life stage versus career stage: A comparative test of the theories of Levinson and Super. *Journal of Organizational Behavior*, 10, 2, April, 117–34.

Osbaldeston, Michael and Barham, Kevin 1992: Using Management Development for Competitive Advantage. *Long Range Planning*, 25, 6, 18–24.

Ouchi, William G. 1981: *Theory Z: How American Business can Meet the Japanese Challenge*. Reading, Mass: Addison-Wesley.

Paddison, Lorraine 1990: The targeted approach to recruitment. *Personnel Management*, November, 54–8.

Palmer, Robin 1983: A sharper focus for the panel interview. *Personnel Management*, May, 34–7.

Partridge, Chris 1990: The right mind for the job. *Daily Telegraph*, 29 November, 22.

Patz, Larry 1975: Performance appraisal: Useful but still resisted. *Harvard Business Review*, 53, May–June, 74–80.

Pedler, Mike, Burgoyne, John and Boydell, Tom 1991: *The Learning Company*. Maidenhead: McGraw-Hill.

Perry, Chad, with Gibson, Bob and Dudurovic Rade 1992: *Strategic Management Processes*. Melbourne: Longman Cheshire.

Peters, Lawrence, O'Connor, Edward, Weekley, Jeff, Pooyan, Abdullah, Blake, Frank and Erenkrantz, Bruce 1984: Sex bias and managerial evaluations: A replication and extension. *Journal of Applied Psychology*, 69, 2, 349–52.

Peters, Tom 1989: *Thriving on Chaos: Handbook for a Management Revolution*. London: Pan.

Peters, T. and Waterman, R. 1982: *In Search of Excellence*. New York: Harper and Row.

Pickard, Jane 1990: When pay gets personal. *Personnel Management*, July, 41–5.

Policy Studies Institute 1991: *Women on the Board*. London: PSI.

Randell, Gerry 1989: Employee appraisal. In Keith Sisson (ed.), *Personnel Management in Britain*. Oxford: Basil Blackwell, 149–74.

Rayner, David 1992: Motivating staff to work themselves out of a job. *Personnel Management*, 24, 2, February, 40–3.

Redman, Tom and Mathews, Brian 1991: *An Empirical Examination of the Adoption of Normative Guidelines in Recruitment Advertising*. Proceedings of the Marketing in Education conference, Cardiff Business School, 2, 904–23.

Redman, Tom and Mathews, Brian 1992a. *The Marketing of Recruitment: An Empirical Investigation of Recruitment Advertising*. Proceedings of the Third Conference on International Personnel and Human Resource Management, Ashridge.

Redman, Tom and Mathews, Brian 1992b. Advertising for effective managerial recruitment. *Journal of General Management*, 18, 2, 29–44.

Redman, Tom and Snape, Ed 1992: Upward and onward: Can staff appraise their managers? *Personnel Review*, 21, 7, 32–46.

Reed, Michael and Anthony, Peter 1992: Professionalizing management and managing professionalization: British management in the 1980s. *Journal of Management Studies*, 29, 591–613.

Resnik, Rob 1991: Psychographics – key to successful recruitment advertising. *The Human Resources Professional*, Winter, 43–47.

Revans, Reg 1987: The learning equation: An introduction. *Journal of Management Development*, 6, 2, 5–7.

Ring, Tim 1992: Efficiency on the line. *Personnel Today*, July, 25–6.

Robertson, Ivan and Makin, Peter 1986: Management selection in Britain: A survey and critique. *Journal of Occupational Psychology*, 59, 45–57.

Rock, Stuart 1990: The hunt for the best hunter. *Director*, November, 74–9.

Rothwell, Sheila 1985: Is management a masculine role? *Management Education and Development*, 16, 2, Summer, 79–98.

Saari, Lise, Johnston, Terry, McLaughlin, Steven and Zimmerle, Denise 1988: A survey of management training and education practices in U.S. companies. *Personnel Psychology*, 41, 731–43.

Sadler, Philip 1989: Management development. In Keith Sisson (ed.), *Personnel Management in Britain*. Oxford: Basil Blackwell, 222–46.

Scase, Richard and Goffee, Robert 1989: *Reluctant Managers: Their Life and Work*. London: Unwin Hyman.

Schein, Edgar H. 1978: *Career Dynamics: Matching Individual and Organizational Needs*. Reading, Mass: Addison-Wesley.

Schein, Edgar H. 1987: Increasing organizational effectiveness through better human resource planning and development. In Edgar H. Schein (ed.), *The Art of Managing Human Resources*. Oxford: Oxford University Press, 25–44.

Schofield, Philip 1981: Getting the Best from Recruitment Agencies. *Personnel Management*, August, 40–3.

Schofield, Philip 1992: Local government job ads: The good, the bad, the ugly. *Personnel Management*, April, 41–4.

Scullion, Hugh 1992a: Strategic recruitment and development of the 'international manager': Some European considerations. *Human Resource Management Journal*, 3, 1, 57–69.

Scullion, Hugh 1992b: Attracting management globetrotters. *Personnel Management*, January, 28–32.

Shackleton, Vivian and Newell, Sue 1991: Management selection: A comparative survey of methods used in top British and French companies. *Journal of Occupational Psychology*, 64, 23–36.

Shepard, Herbert 1958: The dual hierarchy in research. *Research Management*, August, 177–87.

Sidaway, Judith and Wareing, Andrew 1992: Part-timers with potential. *Employment Gazette*, January, 19–26.

Sinclair, Amanda and Hintz, Philippa 1991: Developing managers: Re-examining ten myths about MBAs and managers. *Journal of Management Development*, 10, 7, 53–65.

Sisson, Keith and Storey, John 1988: Developing effective managers: A review of the issues and an agenda for research. *Personnel Review*, 17, 4, 3–8.

Smith, Keith 1989: *The British Economic Crisis: Its Past and Future*. Revised Edition. Harmondsworth: Penguin.

Smith, Mike 1988: Calculating the sterling value of selection. *Guidance and Assessment Review*, 4, 1, 6–8.

Smith, Mike, Gregg, Mike and Andrews, Dick 1989: *Selection and Assessment*. London: Pitman.

Snape, Ed, Redman, Tom, and Wilkinson, Adrian 1993: Human resource management in building societies: Making the transformation? *Human Resource Management Journal*, 3, 3, 1–18.

Snell, Robin 1989: Graduating from the school of hard knocks? *Journal of Management Development*, 8, 5, 23–30.

Sonnenfeld, Jeffrey R. and Peiperl, Maury A. 1989: Staffing policy as a strategic response: A typology of career systems. In Fred K. Foulkes (ed.), *Human Resources Management: Readings*, Englewood Cliffs NJ: Prentice Hall, 67–79.

Stewart, Jim and Hamlin, Bob 1992: Competence-based qualifications: The case against change. *Journal of European Industrial Training*, 16, 7, 21–32.

Stewart, Rosemary 1976: *Contrasts in Management*. Maidenhead: McGraw-Hill.

Stewart, Rosemary 1982: *Choices for the Manager*. Maidenhead: McGraw-Hill.

Storey, John 1992: *Developments in the Management of Human Resources: An Analytical Review*. Oxford: Blackwell.

Storey, John and Sisson, Keith 1990: Limits to transformation: Human resource management in the British context. *Industrial Relations Journal*, 21, 1, Spring, 60–5.

Storey, John, Okazaki-Ward, Lola, Gow, Ian, Edwards, Paul and Sisson, Keith 1991: Managerial careers and management development: A comparative analysis of Britain and Japan. *Human Resource Management Journal*, 1, 3, 33–57.

Super, D. E. 1957: *The Psychology of Careers*. New York: Harper.

Syrett, Michael 1988: Giving job interviews a situational bite. *Sunday Times*, 7 February, 1.

Teel, Kenneth 1978: Self-appraisal revisited. *Personnel Journal*, July, 364–7.

Thomas, Andy, Wells, Martin, and Willard Joyce 1992: A novel approach to developing managers and their teams: BPX uses upward feedback. *Management Education and Development*, 23, 1, 30–2.

Thompson, Marc 1992: *Pay and Performance: The Employer Experience*. IMS Report No. 218, Brighton: Institute of Manpower Studies.

Thomson, Andrew 1992: 10 good things and 10 bad things about MCI. In *Review of Management Education*. London: CNAA.

Thorne, James 1992: New stimulus for those simulations. *Management Today*, December, 66–7.

Tietjen, Carole 1991: Management Development in the NHS. *Personnel Management*, May, 52–5.

Toffler, B. 1986: *Tough Choices: Managers Talk Ethics*. New York: John Wiley.

Townley, Barbara 1990: A discriminating approach to appraisal. *Personnel Management*, December, 34–7.

Trelawny, John 1981: Headhunting. *Personnel Executive*, September, 30–1.

Tsui, Anne and Ohlott, Patricia 1988: Multiple assessment of managerial effectiveness: Inter-rater agreement and consensus in effectiveness models. *Personnel Psychology*, 41, 779–803.

Van Clieaf, Mark 1991: In search of competence: Structured behaviour interviews. *Business Horizons*, March-April, 51–5.

Von Ginlow, Mary 1990: Appraising the performance of professional employees. In Allan Mohrman, Susan Resnick-West and Edward Lawler (eds), *Designing Performance Appraisal Systems.* San Francisco: Jossey-Bass, 196–203.

Walker, James W. 1992: *Human Resource Strategy.* New York: McGraw-Hill.

Wallace, M. J. 1990: *Rewards and Renewal: America's Search for Competitive Advantage through Alternative Pay Strategies.* Scottsdale: American Compensation Association, quoted in Heneman (1992).

Warner, Alan 1990: Where business schools fail to meet business needs. *Personnel Management,* July, 52–6.

Warr, Peter 1993: *Training for Managers.* London: Institute of Management.

Watson, Tom 1989: Recruitment and selection. In Keith Sisson (ed.), *Personnel Management in Britain.* Oxford: Basil Blackwell, 125–48.

Wexley, K. N. and Pulakos, E. D. 1982: Sex effects on performance ratings in manager–subordinate dyads: A field study. *Journal of Applied Psychology,* 67, 433–9.

Wheatley, Malcolm 1992: *The Future of Middle Management: A BIM Report.* London: British Institute of Management.

Whyte, William H. 1960: *The Organization Man.* Harmondsworth: Penguin.

Wiener, Martin J. 1981: *English Culture and the Decline of the Industrial Spirit, 1850–1980.* Cambridge: Cambridge University Press.

Wilkinson, Adrian, Allen, Peter and Snape, Ed 1991: TQM and the management of labour. *Employee Relations,* 13, 1, 24–31.

Williams, Richard 1989: Alternative raters and methods. In Peter Herriot (ed.), *Assessment and Selection in Organizations.* Chichester: Wiley, 725–36.

Wilson, Pauline 1991: Women employees and senior management. *Personnel Review,* 20, 1, 32–6.

Woodley, Carol 1990: The cafeteria route to compensation. *Personnel Management,* May, 42–5.

Wright, Vicky 1986: Does profit sharing improve employee performance? *Personnel Management,* November, 46–50.

Wyche, Chris 1990: *Human Resource Marketing and Communications – the New Horizon?* Paper given at the IPM National Conference, Harrogate.

Index